MORAL
CHOICES

D1595943

MORAL CHOICES

*The Moral Theology of
Saint Alphonsus Liguori*

THÉODULE REY-MERMET, C.Ss.R.

TRANSLATED BY PAUL LAVERDURE

Liguori

LIGUORI, MISSOURI

Published by Liguori Publications
Liguori, Missouri

This book is a translation from the French of *La morale selon saint Alphonse.*

Scriptural citations are taken from the *New Revised Standard Version of the Bible*, copyright 1989 by the Division of Christian Education of the National Council of the Churches of Christ in the USA. All rights reserved. Used with permission.

Library of Congress Cataloging-in-Publication Data

Rey-Mermet, Théodule.
    [Morale selon saint Alphonse de Liguori. English]
    Moral choices: the moral theology of Saint Alphonsus Liguori / Théodule Rey-Mermet : translated by Paul Laverdure.
      p. cm.°
    Includes bibliographical references and index.
    ISBN 0-7648-0233-X
    1. Liguori, Alfonso Maria de', Saint, 1696–1787—Ethics. 2. Christian ethics—Catholic authors. 3. Christian ethics—History—18th century. 4. Catholic Church—Doctrines—History—18th century. I. Title.
BJ1249.R46513 1998
241'.042'092—dc21   98–12012

English Translation Copyright 1998 by Paul Laverdure

Printed in the United States of America

02 01 00 99 98   5 4 3 2 1
First Edition in English

CONTENTS

ABBREVIATIONS

DS   Denzinger-Schönmetzer, S.J., *Enchiridion symbol-
          orum definitionum et declarationum de rebus fidei
          et morum,* 34th ed., Herder, 1967.

DTC   *Dictionnaire de théologie catholique.*

Gaudé   S. Alphonsi Mariae de Liguorio, *Theologia Moralis,*
          critical ed. Léonardi Gaudé, 4 vols., Rome, 1905–
          1912.

Lettere   *Lettere di S. Alfonso M. de Liguori,* ed. F. Kuntz, F.
          Pitocchi, 3 volumes, Rome, 1887–1890.

SH   *Spicilegium Historicum Congregationis SS. Re-
          demptoris,* Rome, 1953– .

Tannoia   Antonio Maria Tannoia, *Della vita ed Istituto del
          Ven. Servo di Dio Alfonso M. Liguori,* 3 volumes,
          Naples, 1798–1802; rpt. Materdomini, 1982.

Vereecke Louis Vereecke, C.Ss.R., *De Guillaume d'Ockham à saint Alphonse de Liguori, Études d'histoire de la théologie morale moderne 1300–1787,* Bibliotheca Historica C.Ss.R. XII, Rome, 1986.

Vidal Marciano Vidal, *Frente al rigorismo moral, benignidad pastoral, Alfonso de Liguori (1696–1787),* PS editorial, Madrid, 1986.

TRANSLATOR'S PREFACE

Alphonsus Liguori's life is well known, but the work which brought him the titles of Doctor of the Church and Patron Saint of Confessors and Moral Theologians is less so. Between the briefest of encyclopedia articles and the multivolume works of the doctor himself, there is practically nothing in English to introduce the interested student to Alphonsus' own thought.

Théodule Rey-Mermet's writings are famous throughout the French-speaking world as an example of clear style and grace. His magisterial biography of Alphonsus, *Le saint du siècle des lumières*, 2nd ed. (Paris: Nouvelle Cité, 1987), was crowned by L'Académie Française and was published in English by New City Press in 1989. At the same time that these books were being published, Rey-Mermet decided to summarize his research and discuss Alphonsus' continuing impact on moral theologians, thinkers, and Christians today in *La morale selon saint Alphonse* (Paris: Les Éditions du Cerf, 1987). When I came across this book some years ago, I immediately thought of a translation for English-language readers.

A few words should be said about the way this book was translated. *Morale* in French can be and has been translated for this book as moral theology, as morality, and even as ethics, depending on the context. Modern readers think and refer to ethics and ethical or nonethical behavior when specialists use the terms moral theology, morality, or immorality. In the same way, universities have gone from teaching courses entitled "Moral Theology" and "Moral Philosophy" to teaching courses on "Religious Ethics" and "Philosophical Ethics." The word morality is used most often today in the field of sexual or religious ethics.

As usual, where English translations and, certainly, English originals were readily available, they were used to replace citations in the French. Saint Alphonsus' ascetical works have been translated into English, most notably in the twenty-two volume Centenary Edition by Eugene Grimm, C.Ss.R. (New York, 1886–1897) and later reedited (Brooklyn, 1926–1928). In many cases, however, because of the scarcity and rarity of any translations, when Rey-Mermet cites the original Latin or Italian, modern English translations have been prepared for this work based on both the original and Rey-Mermet's own interpretation.

I must thank Father Rey-Mermet for kindly granting permission for this translation and for providing corrections of the original French edition so that the English edition would be an improved version. I also thank Dr. Michael Pettem and Dr. Richard Cooper, both of Montreal, for their help during this project.

I hope this book helps others as it did me to know Alphonsus and moral theology better.

PAUL LAVERDURE
MCGILL UNIVERSITY

INTRODUCTION
THE MAN AND HIS WORLD

Alphonsus Maria Liguori was born at Marianella, a suburb of Naples, on the morning of September 27, 1696. Astrology fans may note that he came into the world under the sign of Libra (who holds the scales). Historians may smile at the coincidence because, in actual fact, the baby grew up to be a refined, sensitive, highly gifted, and tireless worker in his profession: the law. As a young man he was a doctor of civil and canon law, an attorney, a judge, and a magistrate. Later, he became a moral theologian of the "just mean" and balanced the scales between law and liberty, the law of God and the rights of human beings, authority and reason, force and conscience, and between grace and free will. Alphonsus' life was a long balancing act as an equiprobabilist. Unique in the Church's history was the Holy See's solemn declaration that in the field of moral theology, Alphonsus Liguori's equiprobabilism marked out a safe path between laxity and rigorism.

DOCTOR OF MORAL THEOLOGY

In the sacristy of the Church of Santa Maria dei Vergini in Naples rests Alphonsus' baptismal register, which anyone may see to venerate. On the margins of page 127 for the year 1696 can be found later and rather unusual annotations. Different hands, in the inks of several periods, have written "Beatified September 1816," "Canonized 26 May 1839," and "Made Doctor of the Church 23 March 1871." But why a Doctor of the Church? In his decree of March 23, 1871, Pius IX praised Saint Alphonsus' great merits as an ascetic and dogmatic theologian, but also clearly pointed out his role as a teacher of morality:

He dispersed the shadows of error spread by unbelievers and Jansenists. Through scholarly works, *and especially through his learned treatises in moral theology,* he threw light on obscure issues and resolved doubts. Through the overgrowth of theologians' opinions that were either too broad or too rigid, he cleared a path along which spiritual directors could safely walk.[1]

This decree was published on July 7, 1871, in the apostolic letter *Qui Ecclesiæ* where Pius IX used similar terms to emphasize the new doctor's victorious struggle for a gentler morality:

When the Jansenist's doctrine had attracted novelty seekers and seduced many minds with the fascination of error and led them astray, God raised up Alphonsus Liguori… who, through his scholarly and exhaustive writings, took to heart the task of clearing the Lord's field of this poisonous weed that had been sown by the powers of Hell.[2]

While this "most zealous Doctor," as the pope called him, is a doctor of prayer and of the Blessed Virgin, for the Church he is nevertheless first and foremost the Doctor of Moral Theology. Pope Pius XII confirmed this seventy-nine years later, on April 26, 1950, by making him the "heavenly patron of all moral theologians and confessors." The pope explained that this title was justified by

an exceptional moral and pastoral teaching, the most highly esteemed in the whole world up to the present time, frequently and strongly recommended by the sovereign pontiffs as a most sure guide for ministers of the sacrament of penance [now called reconciliation] and for spiritual directors.[3]

In an irony of history, the 1950s were to witness a search for new sources and directions in the teaching of moral theology, while the practice of the sacrament of reconciliation would come to a critical turning point. Was the promotion of Saint Alphonsus to the position of patron of moral theologians and confessors merely the last curtain call of a great actor on the Church's stage before he retired finally and forever into the darkness of the wings?

Be that as it may—and only the future can tell—his story remains extraordinary. Besides, let us not exclude a priori the possibility that his story may cast some light on contemporary problems. This book, originally written for the bicentenary of the birth into heaven of the Doctor of Moral Theology and now translated into English for the tricentenary of his terrestrial birth, might serve, we hope, as something more than a eulogy.

The historian of Alphonsus the moral theologian is confronted, however, with a double task. The first task is to place him in the sociological, religious, and pastoral context in which he was immersed and which affected his original thought and action. The second task, of which only Alphonsian specialists have had some knowledge, is to follow the evolution of a constantly changing theology and pastoral ministry over a period of forty years.

But first, who was Alphonsus Liguori? And what was his historical context?

WHO WAS ALPHONSUS LIGUORI?

The life of Alphonsus Maria Liguori (1696–1787), like that of his contemporary Voltaire, who was his senior by a mere two years, covered nearly a century. This century was called the Enlightenment; the century for which Diderot (1713–1784) prophesied the universal domination of science: "Do you see this egg? With it we are going to overturn all the schools of theology and all the temples of the earth."

Naples during this century was a metropolis of a kingdom of the same name, and the third largest capital city of Europe. Only London and Paris were greater.

If any country in Europe has undisputed natural boundaries, it is Italy. Yet Italy is the European nation that took the longest time to reach political unity. In Alphonsus' time, it was still parceled out into some ten sovereign states. The two largest of these—namely, the Papal States and the Kingdom of Naples— were neighbors, and not always friendly ones at that. Alphonsus and his moral theology had an immense struggle to survive in these tumultuous times.

In Naples on September 27, 1696, a child was born a Spanish subject. The Kingdom had been and would be under foreign domination for some time. First Spain; and then from 1707 to 1735, it was Austria's turn. In 1735 the Emperor Charles VI of Austria ceded Naples to Charles de Bourbon. Until dynastic politics brought the Bourbon Charles to the throne of Spain as Charles III, he would be King of Naples, and Naples would know some freedom from foreign rule.

From father to son for centuries, the Liguori family had been knights of Naples. To these knights belonged the task of administering the capital city. The city was divided into six districts or seats, called "sees." The knights made up the "nobility of the see." Their seats were so coveted that the knights accepted only candidates who paid a heavy fee and who were of pure noble descent. From the age of fourteen, the time of entry into office, Alphonsus was councilor for the district of Portanova. He was a magistrate and an administrator. As the minutes attest, from 1710 to 1723, when he was twenty-seven years old, our young official diligently attended the sessions. Our future moral theologian took on all the problems of municipal administration: taxes, feeding the people, setting prices and import-export duties, keeping the property register, noting purchases and sales, farming out communal possessions and privileges, assigning Portanova's church benefices, keeping vital statistics, managing and maintaining streets, plazas, fountains and public buildings, morality, the urban police, and the justices of the peace, and the organization and financing of religious and civic ceremonies. The many problems of the whole lives of an entire people thus called on the young magistrate's abilities and conscientiousness. He learned business administration—and also the misery of the poor, the hardness of the rich, and how the one swindled the other. His "class" and his ability soon earned him flattering responsibilities at the highest level of the Neapolitan *Città* where the deputies of the six districts were seated.

His father, Don Giuseppe Liguori, was the most renowned commanding officer in the navy. The terror of the "Turks," privateers, and blockade-runners, he personified the lion on the family's coat of arms. As admiral of Naples' flagship, he had the entire navy under his command and, in 1709, used the full force of his artillery to relieve Porto Santo Stefano and the

Neapolitan garrisons in Tuscany. He was a man of iron and of ambition. He was even more ambitious for his eldest son than for himself.

Alphonsus was the first of eight children—four boys and four girls—and enjoyed all the privileges of being the first. After advanced studies with eminent private tutors and famous masters in the classics and the arts (painting and music), his father decided that the boy would become a lawyer. Other people's arguments fatten a lawyer's wallet, and the law is the ladder to the top of the bench. The law is money and power rolled into one. Besides, the way to the heights was already open to Alphonsus. His mother, Donna Anna Cavalieri, was the fifth child of one of the Kingdom's chief magistrates, Don Federico Cavalieri, president of the *Real Camera della Sommaria,* both a counting house and a ministry of finance.

Donna Anna had no other ambition than to make her children upright and God-fearing people. She had immediately gone from the boarding school of the *Cappuccinelle Riformate* (Reformed or Strict Cappuccines) to marriage and child-bearing. Her life was one long penitential, prayerful retreat, caring for the poor, and keeping the same canonical hours as the cloister. She also exercised an active, if somewhat anxious, consciousness of her responsibility as the educator of her children. We will return to this last character trait, which became a major influence on our moral theologian.

STUDYING THE GREAT LAWYERS

At the age of twelve, this highly gifted, strong-willed, "hothouse" student had completed a high school course of studies including Cartesian philosophy. In October 1708, he was examined by the Faculty of Law, which held the great Giambattista Vico himself, and was admitted to the study of law.

In a university where Saint Thomas Aquinas had once taught, thirty men now held chairs, but only seven were really professors of university quality, stature, and learning. Fortunately for Alphonsus, four of them taught law: Domenico Aulisio, dean of the Faculty of Civil Law, whom Vico described as "a universal man in languages and the sciences"; Nicola Caravita, professor of feudal law and a Supreme Court judge; Gennaro Cusano and Nicola Capasso, who shared the teaching of the papal Decretals.

The quality of these professors was complemented by the modernity of their methods. Our student was led through the legal forest by guides who left their names carved in legal thought and literature. Abandoning idle speculation to their colleagues in philosophy and theology, they concentrated on the origin and historical development of morality, ethics, and law. They practiced the study of positive law in the same way that positive theology was later practiced. Positive here means historical.

Alphonsus had already learned something of independent thinking and an aversion to specious verbosity from Descartes. From these great lawyers he learned even more and absorbed a feeling for the concrete, the uniqueness of every situation, for the importance of a judgment divorced from any a priori prejudices, for the relative importance of opinions, the differences even among great authorities, the changes in jurisprudence, and the difficult search for "good" in and of itself and the good of all.

On January 21, 1713, when he was just over seventeen years old, our young knight, through an imperial dispensation releasing him from his four remaining years of minority and one semester of courses, was vested in the robes of a doctor of both civil and canon law. In the public defense of his doctorates, he was required to explain, from the Code of Justinian, "the precedence of justice and equity over the letter of the law."

In no more than nine semesters, he had gone through the entire body of civil law, the *Corpus Juris Civilis.* In order to get an idea of the inextricable tangle of laws, ordinances, prescriptions, and privileges that made up the law of the Kingdom of Naples, one must know that for more than twenty-five hundred years the Parthenopian city had never completely been her own mistress. Eleven foreign dynasties succeeded one another, each adding something to the customary local laws. Roman, Byzantine, Lombard, Swabian, Angevin, Norman, Aragonese, Castillian, Austrian, feudal and canon law—eleven bodies of legislation were tangled together. And that is not counting the regional and municipal laws jammed into this maze!

Canon law, the *Corpus Juris Canonici,* had the same diverse origins and a similar proliferation of laws: council canons, papal Decretals, the Decree of Gratien, all huge collections of canons in which it was necessary to separate the wheat from the chaff.

Since that time we have given in to the undoubtedly inevitable temptation to codify as seen in the Swedish code (1734), the Prussian Code (1794), the Napoleonic Code (1804), and the Code of Canon Law (1917, revised in 1983). Codification brings comfortable simplicity, unity, clarity, security, and mastery, but it also tends to deify the law, to transform it into haughty, rigid statutes to which people and circumstances must be sacrificed. Legal compilations, however, required more knowledge, breadth, intelligence, analysis, and subtlety. They allowed for greater personal judgment in weighing opposing opinions, and more flexibility in responding to concrete and unique realities; the law existed for the person, not the person for the law. If I were to compare the two, I should say that in replacing compilation with codification, we moved from the apothecary who measured and varied his medicinal preparations in his laboratory according to tried but flexible formulas to the pharmacist merely distributing standardized manufactured products arranged on the shelves in alphabetical order. Although it was damnation for the ignorant and the despair of legalists, the juridical labyrinth that surrounded Alphonsus was the triumph of the great lawmakers. Their decisions echoed far beyond Italy and were invoked in the courtrooms of the whole Western world. The historian Pietro Colletta wrote: "After the Roman bar, there was never in Europe an order of lawyers more numerous, powerful, rich, and reputed than that of Naples."[4]

A perusal of Alphonsus Liguori's monumental moral theology, the *Theologia Moralis* is enough to reveal how much civil and canonical codes would have simplified his task. But without the fullness and art of the compilations to which his surroundings, his age, and his profession accustomed him over a period of fifteen years, would we have his *Theologia Moralis* at all? At any rate, it would not be such a huge and well-founded body of juridical information, nor would it be adaptable to life's many changes.

Another stroke of luck for our future moral theologian was the fact that in Naples at the time it was unthinkable to practice civil and criminal law without being equally learned in canon law. Indeed, Church law was authoritative in any civil or criminal matters involving a cleric, a nun, a "brother" or, even up to a certain point, any baptized Christian. It regulated not only religion but morals, too. It held exclusive jurisdiction over churches, monasteries, charitable and educational institutions, church lands, and even bandits who sought sanctuary in sacred places.

In this thoroughly sacralized world where ecclesiastical institutions were everywhere, it was almost impossible to find anything that was not "galvanized" by the sacred. Thus canon law had its say in just about every case. It even tended to prevail over civil law. Magistrates and lawyers everywhere ran up against Church courts, the curias: the Roman curias, both distant and local (the nunciature); the archiepiscopal and the royal curias (the Grand Almoner); the diocesan Inquisition; the officiality; and others too numerous to mention.

Should we be surprised, then, that in the early years of the Enlightenment, law, like science, wanted to free itself from the Church's tutelage? Should we blame the state jurists and municipal governments that had for so long run up against the curias and had to bow before them when they succumbed to an anticurial fever and had become regalists, that is to say, partisans of kingdoms with a mature and independent civil society? Thus Alphonsus' teachers, committed Christians though they were, constantly fought for a desacralization of the juridical order. They were respectfully but firmly anticurialist. They formed a militant regalist academy in Caravita's living room, where Alphonsus was a faithful visitor. Their guiding spirit, the patriarch Nicola Caravita, Alphonsus' professor in feudal law, became famous in 1707 with the publication of a rigorous dissertation, the fruit of his scientific and literary conversations: *Nullum jus Romani Pontificis in Regno Neapolitano* ("The Roman Pontiff Has No Legal Rights in the Kingdom of Naples"). It was the historic outcry of an angry anticurialism.

Thanks to this circle of Christians torn between conflicting loyalties, our young lawyer saw the dawn of the Enlightenment.

THE DAWN OF THE ENLIGHTENMENT

Despite the narrow, simplistic view sometimes taken of it, the Enlightenment in Europe—*les Lumières* in France, *Illuminismo* in Italy, *Aufklärung* in Germany, *Ilustración* in Spain—was not limited to the spirit of the *Encyclopédie* and was not everywhere Voltairian. In the preface to his *European Thought in the*

Eighteenth Century (Cleveland, New York: 1963, 1969), Paul Hazard set out "the facts as they were." What did he find?

The scene, as we beheld it, was more or less as follows: first there were the critics in full cry, filling the air with their vociferations. It was the chorus of the new generation upbraiding their predecessors for saddling them with so ill-conceived social order, an order which was the child of illusion and the parent of ill. What had the long process of time resulted in? Disaster. Why, they asked, was this? Thereupon, they openly preferred a charge the like of which for sheer audacity had never before been heard of. Now, the culprit was dragged into open court, and behold, the culprit was Christ! It was more than a reformation that the eighteenth century demanded, it was the total overthrow of the Cross, the utter repudiation of the belief, in other words, in Revelation. What the critics were determined to destroy, was the religious interpretation of life.

Hazard examined these ideas and their failure: "The generations, as they came and went, never bequeathed to their successors anything but the derelict shell of a building....So, in their turn, these newcomers moved on like the rest, leaving behind them, not the order they had dreamed of, but confusion worse confounded." The writer reveals here, however, only one panel of the diptych.

In order to limit our field of investigation—no one could complain that it was too restricted already—we have confined our attention to one particular class or order of minds...the Philosophers and the Rationalists....It were well worth while to study the other collateral branch of the intellectual family... the slaves of desire, the victims of love, earthly and divine, to give heed to their petitions, their appeals...with them to behold the suns that glitter on the fields of night.

"It were well worth while" indeed! As Pierre Chaunu has rightly said:

French thought in the Enlightenment appeared as the militant wing of a movement that it was far from controlling. Thus understood, the thinkers of the Enlightenment are no longer antireligious: theirs is rather a spirit of adaptation and rediscovery.[5]

It was on this construction site that the saint of the Enlightenment took up his tools.

Chaunu strikes another unusual note:

Music dominates the whole of the eighteenth century, and with it the Enlightenment reaches its heights [especially in the theater]. The eighteenth century was passionately obsessed with this great social ritual. [And] for the eighteenth century, theater was opera...born in Baroque Italy at the beginning of the seventeenth century.[6]

To be precise, opera was born in 1606 with *Orfeo* by Monteverdi (1567–1643). And "in the eighteenth century, Naples was the capital of opera,"[7] with Alexander Scarlatti (1660–1725). Moreover, one might well wonder whether in all Naples there was a music lover more enthusiastic about opera than that accomplished musician and harpsichord virtuoso, the young lawyer, Alphonsus Liguori.

Music roots the Enlightenment thinkers in the seventeenth century. This corresponds exactly with Paul Hazard's thesis placing "the crisis of the European consciousness" between 1680 and 1715. This crisis involved a serious questioning of the relations between man and nature, science, art, society, politics, and the Church. Aside from Professor Jean Delumeau in his study of Italy from Botticelli to Bonaparte, most French and even English historians of European civilization appear unaware of the fact that Europe actually exists south of the Alps and of the Pyrenees. The two southern peninsulas, Spain and Italy, nevertheless had their own cultural, artistic, and spiritual highlights. While it might seem that only England, France, and Germany exist, between 1680 and 1730 Naples was fairly bubbling over with a great and innovative liveliness. There was certainly the misunderstood genius of Giambattista Vico (1668–1744), but there was also the entire group of enlightened lawyers who invited and listened to him at Caravita's.

But why lawyers? The answer lies in the fact that the Neapolitan Enlightenment grew mainly out of the lively and universal spirit of the recently deceased and great lawyer Francesco d'Andrea (1625–1698). He had broken free of old intellectual routines and had extended the boundaries of literature, the sciences, philosophy, history, and especially, of course, of his own field, the law. And naturally it was in the realm of the bar and in the law in general that he had the greatest influence. More than elsewhere, one found lawyers who were passionate about language, history, science, literature, philosophy, and politics. Literary journals and books in French, German, and Dutch circulated among them. Far above the dank swamp in which the pettifogging, money-grabbing lawyers croaked, they breathed a purer air of intelligence, culture, and innovative, not to say revolutionary thought. Almost all of them belonged to Nicola Caravita's circle. His son Domenico Caravita was then the presiding judge of the Supreme Court. Alphonsus met them every evening. Gaetano Argento, Costantino Grimaldi, Alessandro

Riccardi, Giambattista Vico, and Pietro Giannone attended—
and left to history their reputations of learning and fame. They
were all Christians, too, as full of faith as they were militant
anticurialists. They fought and wrote for the true freedom of
the Church from its wealth and power. Caravita, Riccardi,
Argento, and Grimaldi were placed on the Index of forbidden
books by Rome and damned to hell by two ambitious Neapolitan canon lawyers who would eventually get to be bishops.
Giannone (1676–1748) sharpened his pen to write the civil history of the Kingdom of Naples, the *Istoria civile del Regno di
Napoli* (published in 1723) and *Triregno* (*The Tiara*), which
earned him excommunication, exile to Geneva, and death in a
Turin prison.[8]

For ten years Alphonsus breathed a heady air sometimes laced
with a whiff of brimstone, if not fire. As one of the foremost
lawyers of the capital, he was no naive boy, but a full partici-
pant. There he learned the freedom of thought that would make
of him an independent and creative moralist. He also acquired
a critical, questioning spirit that no one could shake. He needed
it, because his later life and apostolic activity coincided with a
period in European history when Catholicism was at its lowest
point. He faced deists, materialists, Jansenists, Gallicans, Fe-
bronianists, and regalists, who all cried for death to the Church's
authority. This is the second panel of the Enlightenment diptych,
the one that is the most insolently visible, yet paradoxically
also the darkest.

After two years of clerking, Alphonsus became a full-fledged
lawyer. Between 1715 and 1723 he did not lose a single case. It
is impossible to underestimate what these eight years of litigation taught the future moral theologian about analyzing problems and seeking just solutions. His reputation gained him the
most famous clients and even an international case. During the
spring of 1723, he was offered a case already defeated in a lower

3

court. He thought it just and accepted to appeal it to the Supreme Court. It was an international case in which the Emperor Charles VI himself was implicated. A sum of six hundred thousand ducats was at stake. The opposing parties were the Neapolitan Duke Filippo Orsini di Gravina, nephew of Pope Benedict XIII, and the Grand Duke of Tuscany, Cosimo III de Medici. Orsini, who was closely connected with the Liguoris, had confided this case to the young lawyer who, in spite of his age, had never been beaten. Despite a clearly falsified piece of evidence on the other side, Alphonsus ignored the technical letter of the law and pleaded for equity and justice. But high political influence and bribes had already done their work. In July 1723, when the trial came to an end, the judgment was a foregone conclusion. The lawyer's eloquence and the legal evidence weighed less than a feather in Naples' scales of justice. Flushed with anger, deceived by magistrates he believed incorruptible, ashamed of the legal gown he had worn for ten years, Alphonsus tore off his lawyer's gown and left the court forever, muttering to himself: "World, I know you for what you are." He went to place his knight's sword at the feet of Our Lady of Mercy and enrolled in the archiepiscopal seminary. His father flew into a rage against his son that would last five years.

MORAL
CHOICES

CHAPTER I

MORAL THEOLOGY AND MORAL THEOLOGIANS BEFORE AND AFTER THE COUNCIL OF TRENT

In September 1723, Alphonsus Liguori traded his lawyer's gown for a secondhand cassock taken no doubt from the secondhand clothes closet at his friends, the Oratorians. His father, deeply disappointed, refused to see him again. Luckily for the famous lawyer, his father was usually on his ship, because Alphonsus lived at home and was merely a day-student at the seminary in Naples. He did not even have to take any classes, only private biblical and theological studies under the eminent canon Giulio Torni whom his friend Vico called most learned: *il dottissimo*. In his later writings, Alphonsus would refer to him with affectionate admiration as "my famous and learned teacher."

Reading the *Institutiones philosophicae* of Edmond Pourchot for philosophy, Alphonsus Liguori was, like all thinkers in Naples at that time, a Cartesian. Torni, however, liked to say that he himself "had cut his teeth on Thomism."[1]

Did the teacher turn his student into a Thomist? Thomas

1

Aquinas' friend, Saint Bonaventure was not a Thomist; he was himself. Alphonsus would in the same way become and remain an enthusiastic supporter of his countryman, Saint Thomas Aquinas, and would call him the prince of *theologians*, but never would Thomas be his teacher in philosophy. Alphonsus would never become a Thomist; he would be nothing other than Alphonsian. He would always be more interested in union with Christ, in the preaching of salvation, and in Christian morality rather than in speculation; nevertheless, he could be a deep and rigorous thinker, a formidable dialectician, and a specialist in theological thought. The Dominican Marin-Sola, himself a master of theology, wrote perceptively:

> Although we may ignore the other [eighteenth-century theologians], we must mention the greatest. Quoted chiefly as a moral theologian, Saint Alphonsus has nevertheless enjoyed immense authority on all matters, not only because of his title as a Doctor of the Church, but even more because of the extraordinary impartiality of his theological judgment. He is so completely free from partisanship that it would be difficult to find his equal in this respect except for Saint Thomas and Saint Bonaventure.[2]

His intellectual development grew out of his practice at the bar. It consisted of examining his ideas from every point of view: revelation, the conciliar and pontifical texts, his own meditations, his reading of the masters, the opinions of people around him (and he consulted them a great deal!), his personal experiences, and his prayer. He did not deal in the abstractions of being or nothingness; his philosophy was to know and to make known Jesus Christ, to preach and "to make livable" the Good News of Christ's redemption for the poor. He became a "redemptorist." His development paralleled that of Thomas

Aquinas. They would be so much in agreement that, as Father Sertillanges said: "Rightly understood, equiprobabilism (Alphonsus' moral system) could by all rights be considered a Thomistic solution."[3]

But for the moment Alphonsus is a seminarian. To study dogmatic theology, Torni made him read the *Medulla theologica* of the Lazarist Louis Abelly (1604–1691), a strongly anti-Gallican and anti-Jansenist writer. By an odd contradiction, for moral theology, Torni made him read the *Theologia Moralis* of the rigorist François Genet (1640–1702).

This second theological textbook was part of a tragic and impassioned debate. During his whole life, Alphonsus struggled to stamp out the agony such books caused the Christian West. To understand the debate, we must know a little more history.

SIN AND FEAR IN THE WEST[4]

In the seventeenth and eighteenth centuries, the West subsisted on a diet of religious fear. God was seen as fearsome. Pascal wrote:

> Do we not see that God hates and scorns all sinners, so much so that even at the hour of their death, when they are in their saddest and most pitiful state, divine wisdom will unite mockery and ridicule to the vengeance and fury that will condemn them to eternal punishment: *in interitu vestro ridebo et subsannabo.*[5]

As a consequence of original sin, human nature is entirely corrupt and mired in a diabolical world filled with pitfalls. One must have nothing but contempt for earthly realities. Reason is blind and perverse and can only lead astray. Sin is everywhere; and everyone became obsessed with death, judgment, and hell.

The preachers declared that only a small number were to be saved. Denunciations and condemnations of doctrinal opinions were everywhere.

In 1564, the Index of Forbidden Books was established and swelled. National and diocesan Inquisitions sniffed out heresy everywhere. Views and systems of morality, each claiming to set forth the surest way to an uncertain salvation, clamored for attention. Beginning especially in 1650, moral rigorism and Jansenism spread like fire, leaving behind nothing but more fear: priests refused absolution to the unworthy—and who is worthy? The laity developed an aversion to Communion, reserved to the worthy, and to a small clique of the perfectly worthy, the Jansenists of Port-Royal near Paris, so that heaven would not be entirely empty.

How did this come about?

It goes without saying that sin and penance occupy a large place in both the Old and the New Testaments and in the two-thousand-year history of the Church. One after the other, each kind of atonement and forgiveness that the Church tried were hard: such were the public confessions and penances of antiquity and the financial calculations used to forgive sin between the sixth and ninth centuries. But aside from cases of scandal, they were only proposed not imposed. Until the twelfth century, auricular confession was only *one* of the ways to remit sins, however serious they might be. The Fourth Lateran Council (1215) extended to the whole of Western Christianity prescriptions that had already been promulgated by some regional synods: every faithful Christian henceforth had to confess all of his sins conscientiously at least once a year to his own parish priest. In so doing did the Latin Church forget that the sacramental reconciliation of penitents is not the only usual way to forgive mortal sins? From many specific texts of holy Scriptures, and especially in 1 Peter 4:8, Tradition taught "ten remissions," among which charity that "covers a multitude of sins" is held to be equal to baptism and martyrdom. The following passage from Origen (d. 252) is well known:

Hear how many kinds of forgiveness of sins are contained in the Gospels. The first is that whereby we are baptized "for the remission of sins." The second kind of forgiveness resides in martyrdom. The third is assured by almsgiving. The fourth, when we forgive our brothers their sins....The fifth, when someone leads back a straying sinner.[6]

Two centuries later, around 450, John Cassian in the West echoed Origen at length,[7] thus proving the importance of the doctrine transmitted by this Tradition. Nor is this only a personal opinion. It is still preserved by the Churches of the East, and our Protestant brothers are right to accuse us of not granting it the attention that it deserves. To the above list may be added the purifying role of the Eucharist so strongly attested by a vast number of liturgical prayers and by the theology of Thomas Aquinas. Dare we suggest that the occasional embarrassment of many Catholics in relation to the sacrament of penance represents a reaction of the *sensus fidelium,* the implications of which ought to be carefully weighed? Once again, the institutional approach has swallowed up the others.[8]

Furthermore, a new theory of mortal sin came into being between the Fourth Lateran Council and the Council of Trent. It had previously been called "mortal" because it required penance before admission to the Eucharist. First, even if forgiven by another means, the sinner was henceforth barred from the Eucharist *on pain of sacrilegious Communion* unless the sin had been confessed and absolved, except in cases of necessity.

Second, mortal sin was no longer defined in relation to the sacraments of penance and eucharist but in relation to eternal damnation: "Mortal sin deserves hell." Moreover, a good confession required contrition, or sorrow, a firm resolve not to sin again and, especially, a complete confession of "each and every mortal sin recalled after a serious and accurate examination, and of the circumstances that may alter the type of sin."[9] A confession that does not fulfill all of these conditions is null and—worse—sacrilegious.

From then on, moral theologians, confessors, and penitents tortured themselves in sorting out and classifying the number and types of sins and the circumstances which may or may not alter them. This tallying up finally reached the point that eminent priests and theologians, even as late as the twentieth century, felt crushed by the responsibility and refused to enter the confessional!

Thus sacrilegious confession and sacrilegious Communion became two nightmares haunting all of life, death, and salvation. Pastoral work, both ordinary and missionary, focused on the avoidance or correction of sacrilegious confession. Now a third nightmare began: scrupulosity. "Did I confess my sins, all of them, and properly, with a firm intention to amend?" Since the Western Church barred the way to the other traditional scriptural means for the forgiveness of serious failings, it is not surprising that the road to salvation had become more agonizingly difficult. Delumeau writes:

> Emmanuel Mounier rightly notes that *this syndrome of scruple has historical boundaries. It was unknown to the Eastern church. Even in the Latin West, it does not receive any mention until the moral theologians of the later Middle Ages.* In fact, the Eastern church made no distinction between venial and Deadly Sin, and it never obliged

its adherents to the detailed confession of their offenses. Thus it did not press on to the inexhaustible analysis of cases of conscience. Conversely, the latter—while spurring an extraordinary development of introspection—flourished in the Latin church with the annual and mandatory confession of specific, comprehensively organized sins.[10]

The many agonies caused from this fixation on the confession of mortal sin gave birth to the theory and practice of moral theology.

THE *INSTITUTIONES MORALES*

As we have read, in 1215 the Fourth Lateran Council compelled every faithful Christian to confess his or her sins to that person's own parish priest at least once a year. The poor sinner was caught with red-hot pincers and also threatened with hell's own fire. The parish priest knew exactly who were the white and who were the black sheep in his flock, but the Lateran Council did not portray the confessor as a judge, but rather as a physician for the sick members of his flock. Indeed, it added:

Let the confessor be filled with judgment and prudence in order to know, like a good physician, how to pour "wine and oil" (Lk 10:34) onto the wounds of the injured. Let him inquire carefully into the situation of the sinner and the circumstances of the sin so that he may wisely understand what advice he ought to give and which among the diverse remedies at his disposal he ought to use to heal the sick.[11]

Fortunately, the Fourth Lateran Council also reminded bishops of their duty to preach and to have their diocesan priests go to confession to the bishop or to the bishop's delegates. These delegates were the missionaries of the mendicant orders—the Dominicans and the Franciscans.

The least that could be said is that the Christian populace were in no hurry to go to confession. Still, the law was the law. For their part, the clergy were ill-prepared for their jobs as spiritual doctors. Thus, for more than three centuries, the Dominicans and Franciscans wrote, compiled, and copied confessors' textbooks to help parish priests sort out cases of conscience. The general level of this casuistry was rather legalistic and merely listed what was permitted and what was forbidden.

In 1551, the Council of Trent (1545–1563) promulgated fifteen canons on the sacrament of penance. The hearing of confessions changed from a service of healing to a "judicial act"[12] in which the confessor's questions or medical examination of the patient was replaced by a judicial interrogation requiring a detailed list of charges for which the sinner was responsible: "all his mortal sins, their number, their species and the circumstances that might alter the species." The sinner had to be articulate and knowledgeable. To do his work, the confessor now had to be even more knowledgeable and learned in the law!

In 1563, the Council decreed the establishment of seminaries for the education of the clergy in the humanities, biblical studies, theology, homiletics, and liturgics. Naturally, it emphasized the administration of the sacraments, "above all, that which may be deemed expedient for the hearing of confessions."[13] This was to give preeminence to the sacrament of penance, and, in consequence, to practical moral theology.

In the theological faculties of the universities, especially from the time of Saint Thomas and William of Ockham (d. 1350) a speculative moral theology could be found floating in the ethereal discussions of the most learned scholars. Only the intellectual and social elite of Europe had the means and the time—fourteen years on average—to reach the abstract and technical upper levels of the university curriculum. Moreover, this theoretical moral theology had little to do with the practical, day-to-day ministry among the Christian masses.

At the opposite end of the spectrum, the confessors' *Summas* were often less-than-insightful elementary alphabetical dictionaries. Between the two extremes arose the need for a "confessor's textbook."

The appearance at the dawn of the seventeenth century, 1600 to be precise, of the *Institutiones Morales* of the Spanish Jesuit Juan Azor marks the beginning in moral theology of a new literary genre. Divorced from modern philosophy, dogma, and even speculative moral theology, and likewise a stranger to spirituality and mysticism, this *Theologia moralis practica,* the modest handmaid of the confessor, would henceforth proudly bear the title *Theologia Moralis.*

From that time on, and often serving as a substitute for the study of canon law, moral theology remained faithful to the plan and method defined at the *Collegio Romano* by the framers of the *Ratio Studiorum* (plan of studies).[14]

It is somewhat amusing to note that the *Ratio Studiorum,* published in 1582, gave the following instruction to the Jesuit provincial superiors:

If in the course of studies some students do not pass the year's final examinations with a *mediocriter* [or average mark], thus showing themselves to be unfitted for Philosophy or Theology, they are to be enrolled in the study of Cases of Conscience.[15]

Fortunately, one of the six editors of the *Ratio Studiorum* was Juan Azor (1535–1603), himself a former professor of philosophy and scholastic theology. He quickly took up the challenge to give some dignity to all teachers and pupils of cases of conscience. He began the writing of a kind of textbook of morality that flourished until the Second World War: the *Institutiones Morales* or *Theologia Moralis*.

The *Theologia Moralis* became a weighty book that was studied over the course of two years in the seminary. Students read a treatise on conscience, another on the theological virtues, the Decalogue, the sacraments, contracts, penalties, and the stages of life. Great emphasis was placed on the canon laws that were obligatory under pain of sin.

To solve the concrete cases that arose in the crossfire of life, the treatise on conscience was obviously the most important. The emergence of the modern period—in which humanism, technology, commerce, and banks played a part—multiplied the number of new cases for which solutions had to be invented. The old questions were then asked with greater keenness. What was the difference between what was bad, what was acceptable, and what was perfect? How was salvation gained? What was to be done in cases of persistent doubt? What guide did one follow in a new and upsetting land? scripture? tradition? reason? or experience?

And so began the moral theologians' Four Hundred Years War.

MORALITIES IN CONFLICT

There was a wide range of views among scholars on what was permitted or forbidden or, more precisely, on what a confessor could or could not demand of his penitents. When what is good or necessary is clear, one possesses moral *certitude*. But in doubtful cases, the conscience must be taught to weigh the *probabilities* for or against a particular *opinion*.

Thus *probabilism* was born. Its creator, the Spanish Dominican Bartolomeo Medina (d. 1580), defined it in the following way:

> If an opinion is probable, it is licit [permitted] to follow it even if the contrary opinion is more probable....Every opinion is probable for which there are valid arguments or sound authorities. Such an opinion can be followed without danger of sin.

Why? Because we cannot require anyone to be perfect. Probabilism does not want an in-depth search for truth, but rather a secure conscience. A well-built bridge is safe even if the next bridge is more solid. In the same way, a probable opinion is safe even if a contrary opinion is more probable.

Naturally, a number of theologians in the first half of the seventeenth century slid down the slippery slope. They declared that some opinions were "reliable" although these opinions were, unfortunately, rather quite doubtful and based more on appearances than on sound reasoning. To free themselves from the strictures of the law, instead of Medina's "soundly probable" opinion, these theologians often contented themselves with opinions that were "less probable," "probably probable," and even "not improbable." And what happened to Christian living? It sank into laxism.

From 1640, the excesses of laxism provoked a vigorous reaction that was in principle healthy. But the reaction became excessive and headed in the wrong direction. Blaise Pascal in his *Provincial Letters* (1656) sounded the alarm against casuistry, probabilism, and the Jesuits, all of which he threw together into a vicious hodgepodge. It was ignorant and slanderous to identify laxity with the Jesuits' moral theology of probabilism. Saint Alphonsus himself believed that the "prince of laxists" was the Cistercian Jean Caramuel (d. 1682). Second, people reacted excessively against laxity, because they were blindly led by the heretical teachings of Jansenism.

What was Jansenism? In 1640, there appeared a large book, the *Augustinus*, written some years earlier by the rector of the University of Louvain, Cornelius Jansen, or Jansenius (d. 1638). The work dealt with the doctrine of grace in Saint Augustine. This learned and unfortunate professor, who died as bishop of Ypres, constantly doubted his salvation and believed God to be an awful and despotic deity. He was therefore in a suitably dark mood to read Augustine, who was himself rather pessimistic about everything. Jansenius seized on the most pessimistic of Augustine's propositions: free will does not exist, thus human beings are incapable of doing any good; grace alone acts; moreover, Christ did not die for everyone: from out of the "damned mass" of humankind, God arbitrarily chose certain privileged souls to whom he grants eternal salvation and to no one else.

Jansenius' friend, Duvergier de Hauranne, the abbot of Saint-Cyran (d. 1643), introduced this tragic Christianity to his penitents, the nuns of Port-Royal-des-Champs in Paris. The nuns and hermits of Port Royal became Jansenists.

With its theology of an arbitrary God jealously guarding heaven, Jansenism could only infuse anxiety, an obsession with the divine law, the requirement of angelic purity, and a fearful withdrawal from God's sacraments—in a word, moral and pastoral rigorism to all noble souls.

Father Vereecke writes:

What did the Jansenists teach in moral theology? Passing over the nuances of each writer, we can characterize all of Jansenist morality as follows. The only source for Christian life is tradition, that is to say, Holy Scriptures interpreted according to the simple rules of the Church Fathers, and above all Saint Augustine. God's will is revealed there and in the conscience of the faithful illuminated by the Holy Spirit. All of morality consists in knowing the will of God. Jansenist morality is always a leap of faith toward God, because reason, corrupted by original sin, can never really know morality as it cannot know dogma. All ignorance or error in the moral realm is at once a result of original sin and the sin of a faithless conscience. The one and only conflict is between a corrupted nature and the will of God, and the solution to the conflict is entirely clear. So, Jansenism rejected probabilism as "moral Pelagianism" [relying on the individual's will] and sought to establish an absolute tutiorism [certainty]. The Word of God, as it was embodied in the primitive Church, applied with unmitigated rigor without regard to the circumstances of time and place, was the Jansenist ideal morality.[16]

Note that the sources of Jansenist morality were exclusively biblical, patristic, and mystical; they excluded reason, experience, and the writings of recent authors. This is almost the opposite of Alphonsus' approach, which granted priority to reason and experience and, aside from Saint Thomas, relied only on post-Tridentine authors. While Alphonsus was always guided by the Scriptures in other areas, he rarely used it to resolve cases of conscience.

As soon as it appeared, *Augustinus* drew vehement protests from the Jesuits of Louvain and shortly from everywhere else. It was praised, however, by bishops, the "religious" Orders—such as Bérulle's Oratorians, the Dominicans, and the Carmelites—and university professors. Rome's repeated condemnations of Jansenism in 1641, 1647, 1653 and above all by the papal bull *Unigenitus* in 1713 did little more than spread the disease throughout Europe, inflame the anti-Roman complex, and spark new conflicts between Catholics.[17] Indeed, Catholics were divided into two opinions, even two schools. On one side were those who were concerned before anything else with defending the God's sovereignty—his omnipotence, his rights, and his law. For them God was everything, did everything, could do everything; humanity was nothing, did nothing, could do nothing. On the other side were those who also wished to honor the human person who was "made in the image of God" and possessed reason, will, and freedom. Those who followed Saint Thomas Aquinas—the Dominicans, the Holy Office, and most bishops and seminaries—were impressed with Jansenism's logic and formed the first school. The Jesuits, the followers of Saint Ignatius of Loyola and their Spanish theologian, Luis Molina (1535–1600), made up the second school. For brevity's sake, we can speak of Thomists and Molinists.

The Thomists cast themselves in the role of knights protecting God's sovereignty. According to their theology, grace accomplishes everything. According to their moral theology, when in doubt, it is always necessary to abide by the most probable (*probabilior*) opinion and even to adopt the most certain (*tutior*), that is to say, to take the side of the law. They were therefore *probabiliorists*, often *tutiorists*, and always *rigorists*.

In the opposing camp, Molinists believed that, after all, God is entirely free to let humanity participate in his sovereignty. Human decisions work with grace in salvation. In Molinist morality, human freedom has its own rights, willed by God. One may go against the law, and follow any probable (*probabilis*) opinion. They were therefore *probabilists*, liberals, and often accused of *laxism*.

The second half of the seventeenth century witnessed the

rigorists' growing triumph almost everywhere. In spite of the Index and the fires condemning both to hell, *Augustinus* and, later, the *Provincial Letters* succeeded in spreading Jansenism, because the official climate also blew a gale of severity against the permissiveness springing from the Renaissance. Alexander VII in 1665 and 1666 and Blessed Innocent XI in 1679 succeeded in strangling laxity with their condemnations. Moreover, the latter pope almost dealt a death blow to probabilism in singling out the following statement for a special condemnation: "I consider it probable that the judge can pronounce sentence by following an even less probable opinion."[18] The pope then had the Spanish moralist and probabiliorist Father Tyrso Gonzalez (d. 1705) elected as General of the Society of Jesus, and entrusted him with the task of imposing the probabiliorist system on the Jesuits.

Alexander VIII, the pope who followed Innocent XI, intervened, however, to make sure that probabilism was not entirely strangled. In 1690, he condemned many of the presuppositions of Jansenism as well as tutiorism. The new Jesuit General, Tyrso Gonzalez, "failed in his efforts, and throughout the eighteenth century many Jesuits remained faithful to a balanced probabilism stripped of laxist or risky opinions."[19]

But owing to the "liberties of the Gallican Church" of France, the 1690 Roman decree remained a dead letter north of the Alps. An assembly of the French clergy meeting at Saint-Germain in 1700 ended the century, le *Grand Siècle*, by condemning probabilism in all its forms. This was done without appeal and without the smallest murmur of a protest. On the contrary, bishops, seminary teachers, preachers, and confessors within France and beyond, even as far away as Canada thought that the honor of God required confessors to see sin everywhere and to treat sinners harshly. Sex between spouses, for example, was declared culpable unless it was justified by the will to procreate or was excused in one who claimed that the other party demanded his (rarely her) conjugal right. The recommended remedy for sinners was to refuse absolution and, consequently, Communion. It was too dangerous to leave medicine where the sick could get at it and abuse it!

On the eve of Saint Alphonsus' entry onto the scene, what was the situation of moral theology? Probabilism, often accused of laxism, was in noticeable retreat. Rigorism, by claiming to represent the radical requirements of the Gospel, was adopted by shepherds of souls and locked Christians into a stifling and pitiless prison. But, more than anything, confusion reigned everywhere. Opinions that were probable, less probable, more probable, equally probable, probably probable faced and cancelled each other out. Shepherds of souls, and even more the souls themselves, got lost in the forest of opinions. On the horizon, one could still glimpse the great choices between sin and divine grace and the choices Christians had in their relationships with God and the world.

In all of this confusion, was it possible to work out a moral theology that would not compromise the requirements of an authentic Gospel and, at the same time, pay attention to the new conditions facing individuals and Christian communities? This is what was at stake in the controversies surrounding moral theology. This was the great question that Saint Alphonsus Liguori would try to answer in his *Theologia Moralis*.[20]

16

CHAPTER 2

ALPHONSUS LIGUORI'S TEACHERS

A new history of moral theology cannot merely be satisfied with the study of the published works of the great moralists. It must also consider the education, context, life, and development of the authors of these works.

This is true of Alphonsus Liguori more than of any other. His long life—ninety-one years—is an exceptional fact in itself. His publications on morality extend over thirty-nine years (1746–1785). His thinking, beginning with his seminary days, would continue to evolve until 1762. His research would keep him busy until 1779 when he was eighty-three.

But let us begin at the beginning. Who were his teachers in moral theology?

"MY MOTHER'S TENDER CARE"

Captain Liguori was not easy on his son. For example, one night a week he would make him sleep on the bare stone floor; he would lock and bolt him in with his harpsichord teacher for three hours at a time. But the father's profession often kept him at the docks or on the high seas. Thus, almost the whole of the child's education fell to his mother.

She could have turned it over to others. But having left the secluded life of the *conservatorio* only at the age of twenty-five, this great lady would remain a woman of duty to the point of scrupulousness. Father Antonio Tannoia, Alphonsus' biographer, also knew her and wrote:

Alphonsus' early education was not entrusted to servants, as was most often the practice among the nobility. Rather, his own mother took complete and exclusive charge of it. Fully aware of her obligations, Donna Anna made it entirely her business. She did not let anyone else teach this son, or his brothers and sisters, his Christian duties....She was careful not to let them associate with fellows of their own age. And in order that grace might ward off evil and that her children might early acquire the habit of hating sin, each week she led them to the church of the Oratorians to confess to Father Tommaso Pagano, her own confessor and a relative of theirs.[1]

Alphonsus would remain tenderly grateful to his mother for having protected him and armed him against sin. He often liked to say: "If I did nothing evil in my youth, I owe it entirely to my mother's care."[2]

But every good thing has its cost. Alphonsus' tenderness of conscience and moral innocence would for a long time keep him on the verge of scrupulosity. His initial adherence to the official rigorism, followed by his "compulsory" probabilism can only be understood in any depth by paying attention to his sensitivity—to his being so easily affrighted by even the shadow of sin. This same applies to his reliance on obedience, the only firm guarantee for those assailed by scruples.

"COPIOSA REDEMPTIO"

In Naples, Christ's Passion was the object of an intense and demonstrative devotion. Captain Don Giuseppe Liguori had in his ship's cabin four statuettes of the passion of Christ to which he entrusted the salvation of his soul, his life, and his ship. His son, a twenty-three-year-old lawyer and already a mystical painter, has left us a stirring painting of Christ dead on the cross. The Savior's face, showing no tortured anguish, instead radiates love, peace, and hope: passionate love for sinners, peace between God and all people, and hope in an abundant, already achieved Redemption.

"Copiosa apud Eum"—"And with Him is plenteous redemption" (Psalm 130:7). This was the motto that Alphonsus would give to his missionary congregation as a striking denial of Jansenist pessimism. He would write ten works of varying lengths on the Passion. Chronologically, his first work on morality was an attentive contemplation of God who had died because of love for an unfortunate world. From the beginning of his ministry, the contemplation of the crucified Jesus made it impossible for him, in spite of official instructions, to refuse forgiveness and absolution to any penitent.

Nor, as is well known, did he separate the Savior from the Mother of Mercy. He began his *Glories of Mary* nearly a decade before undertaking his *Moral Theology*. In the former we read:

And what mother would not deliver her son from death if it only depended on her asking the favor to obtain it from the judge? And can we think that Mary, who loves her clients with a mother's most tender love, will not deliver her child from eternal death when she can do it so easily?[3]

"I WAS A LAWYER"

Was there ever in the history of the Church a moral theologian as experienced in the law, both civil and canon, and its procedures as Alphonsus Liguori? Or one whose judgment and sense of justice had been more sharpened in the study of so many jumbled collections? For fifteen years he was a full-time jurist, first as a student, then as a probationer, magistrate, and next as a counsel in the most famous courts after Rome of all Europe.

This preparation was providential for Alphonsus' later scholarly work as a moralist....It gave him the broad and deep judicial learning that supports his ethical constructions. Moreover, such practical training gave him an insider's true perspective of moral acts and showed him how they can be judged in the light of Christian wisdom.[4]

Besides, even though moral and civil law sometimes made odd bedfellows—what is legal may be immoral—it is often the case that the law binds the conscience. As for ethics and ecclesiastical legislation, they are twin sisters—if not more than twins. Both lawyers and spiritual directors composed the *Confessors' Summae*. In 1740, Cardinal Lambertini, the future Pope Benedict XIV to whom Alphonsus dedicated his *Moral Theology,* observed:

For a long time holy theology has been closely united with canon law. Indeed, in substance most of the canons are only conclusions drawn from theological principles. In this sense, Jean Gerson made the excellent remark: If looked at clearly, the canons are only corollaries of the Gospel and other sacred books—corollaries deduced by those to whom Christ said, "Who hears you hears me." Why should it then be surprising that those who were in charge of the study of principles should also be those who knew and promulgated the legislative conclusions?[5]

Lambertini, it is true, wrote three years before Alphonsus Liguori undertook his major work. But, in fact, theology and law maintained their alliance. The 1983 *Code of Canon Law* enters into theology at Canon 204 and does not leave it until Canon 1254. Hence, if one recalls the constant struggles between civil and canon law under the *Ancien Régime*, one cannot take too lightly the reminder that our moralist once gave to one of his spiritual sons: "I was a lawyer."[6]

"ALL PROFESSORS OF RIGORISM"

It is impossible to fathom why Giulio Torni gave Liguori the seminarian both fire and water, as it were: Abelly for dogma and Genet for moral theology. Louis Abelly, bishop of Rodez and a friend and disciple of Saint Vincent de Paul, had published a rigorously orthodox, anti-Gallican, and anti-Jansenist *Medulla theologica* in two volumes (1650, 1651). Torni preferred this textbook because, as a Thomist and a good teacher, he appreciated the Cartesian method of "clear and distinct ideas." Many years later at the age of eighty-five, Alphonsus wrote on January 17, 1782, to Father Di Costanzo, who was in charge of philosophy students, that "when the time comes to move into philosophy, go with Abelly. Monsignor Torni made a great deal of Abelly, because this author is clear, very methodical, and exact."[7]

Torni no doubt appreciated Abelly's doctrine, including, as we shall see, his pastoral doctrine. Against the Jansenists, Abelly maintained that God wishes to save everyone and gives to each person a grace sufficient to observe the commandments. Attrition (imperfect contrition) is enough to obtain absolution for the forgiveness of serious sins. Do not impose heavy penances, and do not refuse absolution to a poor backslider who is well disposed. To go to Communion, it is enough to be free of mortal sin.... Alphonsus Liguori fought through thick and thin to restore this traditional doctrine, which is accepted today without question. In fact, the Jansenists detested Abelly. In 1686, Antoine Arnauld wrote: "He is an out-and-out miserable attritionist, probabilist, and sufficientist author....And yet his will soon be the only book read in seminary.[8] Arnaud hardly knew how right he was. Abelly's work would be republished for two centuries.

But by what stupefying contradiction did Torni place Genet's *Morale de Grenoble* in the hands of his student? It portrayed another God, relied on a different Gospel, and came from a different Church!

Why was his work of moral theology named after Grenoble? François Genet was born in Avignon, then the capital of the Comtat Vanaissin, a possession of the Holy See. Genet was a subject, not of the king of France, but of the pope, but after he preached a mission in Grenoble, Bishop Le Camus asked him to prepare a moral theology textbook for his seminary. His *Morale de Grenoble* would warp innumerable generations of priests in France, Germany, and Italy.

The first two volumes appeared in Paris in 1676 under the title *Théologie morale ou Résolution des cas de conscience selon l'Écriture Sainte, les Canons et les Saints Pères* (*Moral Theology*, or *The Solution of Cases of Conscience, according to the Holy Scriptures, the Canons, and the Holy Fathers*). This praiseworthy-looking title

was a theological position that clearly revealed Genet's Jansenist tendency. Human nature has been so corrupted by original sin that our will, already inclined to evil, further darkens our mind in moral matters in such a way that the mind cannot rightly choose between moral acts. Thus, in order to resolve cases of conscience, Man absolutely needs Revelation, that is, Holy Scriptures interpreted by Tradition. Man cannot appeal to reason. This was a direct condemnation of probabilism and the moral pursuit as it had been carried on by moral theologians since at least the Council of Trent.[9]

According to the five bishops who supported Genet's book, this was just what was needed to purge "moral laxatives." Thus Genet was encouraged, protected, and promoted. A priest writing under the pseudonym Jacques Remonde denounced Genet's rigorism in two volumes of *Remarques* (1678). He soon regretted it, because the Holy Office placed the *Remarques* on the Index and declared Genet's *Théologie morale* free of error in 1679. The Master of the Pope's Sacred Palace, Capizucchi, struck the official Roman note: "This theology is excellent. Its doctrine is healthy, solid, safe, and necessary for the correction of morals." What are we waiting for to put the bishop's crozier in the hand of such a vigilant priest? He was only thirty-seven years old! Blessed Innocent XI quickly named him theological canon of Avignon in 1677; then on March 18, 1686, bishop of Vaison (called *la Romaine* at the beginning of the twentieth century). Seven days later he was consecrated to the episcopate in Rome in the Church of Saint Augustine. Augustine, *Augustinus*—a coincidence? That same year Bishop Le Camus, who had raised up this purifying light in the Church, was rewarded with the cardinal's red hat.

But the rigor that had gained Canon Genet the miter soon led him to a kind of martyrdom. Versailles and Rome were at loggerheads. Since the bishop of Vaison had welcomed into his diocese the *Filles de l'Enfance de Jésus*, a congregation that had been suppressed in Provence because of its Jansenism, Louis XIV who had once again invaded the Comtat, had the bishop arrested, and imprisoned at *Île de Ré* for many long months. This sincere, zealous, pious, and rigorist prelate died in 1702, carried away by a river he tried to cross coming home from a retreat at the monastery of Bompas.[10]

Two years before he became a bishop, he had completed the eighth volume of his great work. As a supreme honor, he saw Bossuet adopt it for his seminary at Meaux, and all the clergy of France drew their inspiration from it for their assembly of 1700.

We know that at least the first two volumes were sent prior to publication for corrections and editing to Antoine Arnauld, a staunch Jansenist. The Jansenists therefore had nothing but praise for this sacred tome. In it, the confessor was urged to severity above all: severity in examining the penitent; severity in granting—no!—in refusing absolution. The work devotes thirty pages to inciting the priest to deny the forgiveness of a God who commanded people to forgive one another seventy times seven. It recommends deferring absolution until the sinner has experienced something of the eternal pains merited by his sins—and until the sinner was humbled. James Pollock writes: "Genet's goal was to reduce the penitent to contrition by humiliating and breaking him."[11] May the penances fall thick and fast! As for Communion, it required such conditions that it was better to avoid it altogether. Thus

one ought not to advise a person to go to Communion after he has fallen into mortal sin, even if he is contrite and humbled [and, of course, absolved]. [He must] rather abstain for some time because of the respect owed this great sacrament.

And all of this was backed up by the grimmest quotations selectively culled from the Fathers and the Councils.[12]

Such a "healthy" work could not but be exported for the benefit of the whole Catholic world. Thus it was translated into Latin (1702–1703) and published in Paris and four times in Venice with a dedication to Pope Clement XI. Approved by more than one hundred and sixty Italian councils or synods, it was soon followed throughout the peninsula, beginning in Rome.

That is how we come to find Genet's *Moral Theology* in the hands of Alphonsus and the teachers and students of Naples' seminary.

We have spent so much time on this work because it reveals the official extent of rigorism in the Church that Alphonsus entered. It allows us to understand the initial moral orientation of our seminarian, as well as the dramas of conscience into which it threw him, the stroke of genius that would lead him to swim against this stream, and the energy he would have to spend throughout his life to reverse it throughout the Church. He himself wrote in 1764:

> I would have you know that from the beginning of my ecclesiastical studies I was directed by teachers, *all* of whom professed the rigorist doctrine. The first moral theology book they put into my hands was Genet, leader of the probabiliorists. For a long time even I was a stubborn partisan of probabiliorism.[13]

Besides, Naples was ready to give Genet a very warm welcome. As far back as 1646, Don Sansone Carnevale, a famous Neapolitan priest, had established the most illustrious of the diocesan mission societies in the capital, the Apostolic Mission Society (whose members were called the *Illustrissimi*).

Carnevale was a champion of rigorism. The rest of the clergy, Molinists and probabilists all, however, did not follow him or his society, until the arrival of Cardinal James Stuart (Giacomo Cantelmo to the Italians) as archbishop in 1691. A reformer with an iron hand, he reinstituted the diocesan Inquisition and narrowly missed being run out of the *Città* by the more tolerant authorities.[14] During the eleven years of his episcopate (1691–1702), he restored Saint Augustine and Saint Thomas to their usual places of honor and required that the seminary and the clergy rally round probabiliorism.[15] To promote this reform, he relied on a zealous agent, Canon Biagio Visconti, whom he had personally converted to Saint Augustine. Visconti made a public retraction of his former "errors" and wrote a *Synthesis... moralis* in which he maintained, for example, that ignorance of the law is no excuse for sin and that the opinion that favors the law must always take precedence, even if it is less probable than the opinion that favors liberty. This meant, in effect, the enslavement of reason and the individual! Stuart's successors, cardinals Francesco Pignatelli (1703–1734) and Giuseppe Spinelli (1735–1754), would also trim their sails to the winds of rigorism.[16]

And what of Alphonsus' teacher, Don Giulio Torni? One might surmise that this fervent follower of the "soft Abelly" (as Boileau described him) was not a very severe rigorist since he gave the antidote at the same time that he made Alphonsus drink poison. But it can hardly be doubted that like "all the seminary professors" he was indeed a rigorist. In writings dating from 1762 and from 1765 Bishop Liguori wrote:

> I am telling you the truth: when I began the study of moral theology I was initiated into it by a teacher of the strict doctrine. I also began by hotly defending the same point of view.[17]

Educated by the Dominican Gregorio Selleri, then Master of the Sacred Palace, "Torni reveals the strictest tutiorism in the notes accompanying his edition of the *Commentaries of Estius*" (Cacciatore). Rome and Naples' cardinals sided with Genet. The doctrine that was imposed on the Neapolitan seminary, of which Torni was the intellectual head, the doctrine which officially ruled in the Apostolic Missions, of which Torni was frequently a superior, and that which was adhered to by an "infinite number" of Neapolitan priests, was probabiliorism. Moreover, being the "official theologian of His Eminence, the Cardinal," how could Torni not share the theology and pastoral strategy of Naples' cardinal archbishops who, from Cantelmo to Spinelli, were militant rigorists?

"Men of Great Wisdom"

Still, it may seem to us that Alphonsus is full of contradictions. In his second year of seminary (1724), he had become one of the *Illustrissimi*. He gave several missions a year with them and worked side by side with Torni, not in theory and books, but in action on the missions. Not yet a priest, the young missionary preached to the crowds and catechized the children. Naturally, he could not hear any confessions. Thus he had no problem in "vigorously defending a strict doctrine." But through many questions and conversations he undoubtedly saw that Torni's official intellectual convictions softened in contact with real, flesh-and-blood people.

Alphonsus was ordained a deacon on April 6, 1726. The archbishop immediately delegated the former lawyer to preach throughout the capital. The fashionable churchgoers of Naples as well as the *lazzaroni* (outcasts or beggars) in the squares and streets of the slums, whom he was going to evangelize, were overwhelmed by his sermons and waited impatiently for him to hear their confessions. Ordained a priest on December 21, 1726, he could at last welcome them—but such was not to be the case. The new priest did not take his place in the confessional for a year. Was this because the archbishop delayed granting him faculties? On the contrary, Alphonsus himself refused to sit on this tribunal where he knew there was more rigor than mercy.

Personally inclined to scruples, Alphonsus was in no hurry to grant easy absolutions, and even less to refuse them in the name of the doctrine, which as a seminarian he had vigorously defended. It took a formal order from Cardinal Pignatelli reminding him of the obedience that every priest vows to his bishop on the day of his ordination to get him to take the plunge. Only in December 1727, a full year later, did Alphonsus present himself before the synodal jury appointed to examine his fitness. The archbishop hastened to grant him the faculty of hearing the confessions of all types of penitents throughout the diocese. He was trembling as he entered the confessional, fearing that he would be torn apart by two ropes pulling him in opposite directions: the first rope representing the doctrine of severity and the second the tenderness of Christ, who died for sinners. It was to be his greatness that as a young probabiliorist priest he never refused an absolution, but at the cost of numberless prayers and tortuous exhortations.[18] And at the cost of extraordinary fear and anguish until, one day, a light broke through.

Torni's case gets a little more complicated at this point, but it helps us to understand Alphonsus. In three different Latin *Dissertations* published in 1749, 1755, and 1762, and in nearly identical sentences, Father Liguori made what is at first sight, a rather astonishing declaration about the period following his seminary studies:

Later, after I had applied myself to the missionary apostolate, I realized that the gentler doctrine was followed by many men of great wisdom and probity, beginning with my teacher, the illustrious and very learned Don Giulio Torni.[19]

Was Torni a hypocrite? And what of the Oratorian Tommaso Pagano, Alphonsus' spiritual director from early childhood? His friend Canon Giuseppe Iorio of the diocesan congregation founded by the Jesuit Pavone? Father Tommaso Falcoia, former Superior General of the Pious Workers, the *Pii Operarii*? And that luminary of God, the Dominican Ludovico Fiorillo? What of Alphonsus' early companions, Giovanni Mazzini, Cesare Sportelli, Paolo Cafaro; and later, the young and erudite Basilian priest Giuseppe Muscari, who would give him some trouble later still? These are people to keep in mind, as well as other men of great wisdom.

These men were no hypocrites, but rather men playing different roles in different situations. As is well known: the role of a preacher is one thing; the role of a confessor is something very different. The missionary is "a lion in the pulpit and a lamb in the confessional." The teacher and the preacher require high ideals because it looks good in the eyes of the authorities and because one has to try to get the best out of the faithful. The confessor, however, must be prepared to welcome the faithful with all their ordinary weaknesses, as one gathers up the wounded and dead after a battle that one had hoped would have been heroically triumphant. The ideal and the real are two seemingly contradictory attitudes, but they each describe two complementary ministerial functions in the service of the people of God.

But there are also bureaucrats who think up and draft official texts—and textbooks of morality. They make up the party line and the government apparatus. In each of Alphonsus' *Dissertations* cited previously, he lets us follow his progressive discovery. He continues in these words:

> Still later I realized that the strict doctrine had only a few teachers and few followers. They were, moreover, all more devoted to speculation than to the ministry of the confessional.

They were men of the governing curias and professorial staffs—theoreticians of moral theology enclosed in ivory towers—scholars and administrators far above the ordinary ministry in the lives of the poorest people. Certainly they were dutiful priests, but they were idealists rather than realists. They hid behind their principles instead of mingling with the masses. And they possessed power. In a Christendom where no one could escape their spiritual power, they became easily intoxicated on the rights of God and his law. Had the Lord not asked them as he did John the Baptist to "prepare a perfect people?"[20] People like Vincent de Paul and Abelly who devoted themselves to popular missions lived, as did the Christ of the Gospels, among ordinary people. When one was in constant touch with life and sinful human beings, it was necessary either to spit out rigorism or to abandon the ministry.

Torni did neither the one nor the other. A big wheel in the official machine and a missionary superior, he seems to have "done the splits" by assigning and teaching Genet in the seminary, but then ignoring Genet on the missions. While Genet was required in the seminary, Torni chose to follow Jesus Christ on the missions. If one were inclined to joke about these matters in which the image of the Church and the salvation of human beings were played off against each other, one might recall Jacques in Molière's *Miser,* who is both coachman and cook and who in turn puts on his coachman's livery or his apron depending upon whether Harpagon calls for one or the other. Joking aside, Torni was no doubt a priest torn into two, yet great enough to satisfy the episcopacy on the one hand while gaining the trust and the veneration of his disciple on the other.

Torni's duplicity, which Alphonsus Liguori observed with surprise and relief, played out between the bishops and Rome's official policy on the one side, and the pastoral strategies of "many men of great wisdom" on the other, created a sad schism within Catholicism similar to those with which we are familiar today.

Alphonsus did not remain resigned to the situation. Trained by Descartes to give weight to the authority of teachers only according to the weight of their arguments, he moved from academic theories to lived realities. It was one thing to hold in one's hands a textbook of morality and quite another to clasp the saving Blood, to give or to withhold it from actual sinners for whom Christ died out of love. When it is a question of saying to a brother in the name of probabiliorism, "You will do this or not do that, no matter what the cost, on pain of exclusion from the sacraments and threat of eternal damnation," one feels far less sure than one does in one's study of the importance of casuistical reasoning. Alphonsus often said: "How dreadfully wrong it is to say, 'You are damned. I cannot absolve you!' We are forgetting that this person was redeemed by Christ's Blood!"[21]

Nevertheless, a man inclined to scruple[22] is unlikely to move from rigorism to leniency as one changes one's shoes or hat. This is truer still when the official Church recommended Genet to him and he has absorbed this teaching for a long time. Torn between the *Morale de Grenoble* and the Gospel of Christ, he was to experience a long struggle with scrupulousness in which he would be reduced to relying upon the "men of great wisdom" who had opened his eyes. At this point, Alphonsus Liguori's *Notebook of Conscience* begins to enlighten us about his inner development as a moral theologian.

Beginning in 1726, Alphonsus kept in his pocket a small parchment-bound notebook, 4.5 by 2.5 inches (113 by 65 mm) to jot down and remember things. If he wanted to write a note to himself, he would open the book at random and scribble in his thin handwriting a few short, abbreviated paragraphs, names, numbers, unfinished sentences, or mysterious—often incomplete—words. The same little page could hold lines written five or six years apart. Some seventy-five dates, from 1726 to 1743, scattered throughout the notebook do not even allow us to date all of these fragments. Only a careful study of the content, ink, and handwriting suggests an approximate chronology. Many passages were completed or revised at a later date.

What are the contents of this valuable document? It comprises financial accounts, sermon outlines, some verses, lists of names, liturgical formulas, faculties granted by bishops, an outline of the Redemptorist Rule, even a recipe for a *balsamo simpatico*. Above all, however, there are matters of conscience, as the title he himself wrote at the beginning of this spiritual notebook indicates—*Cose di coscienza*. These consist of personal problems and decisions he received from his spiritual directors, resolutions, prayers, discussions of cases of conscience, and pastoral directives. It is sometimes difficult to decide whether a particular paragraph concerns himself or is a remark from the moralist about his penitents. Some passages are underlined or written in capital letters. Many others remain and will remain mysteries to us. That is why the projected publication of this intimate notebook necessary for an understanding of Father Liguori may never come about and may never tell us more than we already know.[23]

We shall return later to this very important document. For

now, here are a handful of sentences illustrating Alphonsus' crisis.

Pagano, with Torni and Burr.[?] [told me]: let the confessor act freely every time he does not have contrary evidence.

And Torni: the formal principle of absolving, do freely what comes immediately to mind....Confirmed by Pagano, in cases of hesitation to do what I wish unless it is clear that it is wrong...then, even if in great fear [of making an error], to act thus is not a sin, but a useful precept for acquiring in the direction [of souls] the confessor's necessary freedom, it being always understood that one does not wish to offend God in suchwise.

Order never to consult [after the fact] about what has been done. Torni. Only ask for advice about doubtful cases full of [complicated] circumstances and of great importance. But when you have some probability on your side, act freely.
N.B.—Confirmed May 1728. [p. 17]

Do not ask any questions unless you have good reason to think that the penitent has not confessed everything. Usually, except for this, do not interrogate. [p. 19]
Pagano...replied to me that I should follow a probable opinion in preference to a more probable one. [p. 26]
Don Cesare [Sportelli], that obedience gives me as my spiritual Father, asks me as a case of conscience to act differently: (1) to follow the probable opinion when another is more probable; (2) no longer to ask myself whether my spiritual Fathers were probabilists [when they advised me], but simply to obey them. [p. 39]

It was again recalled that we can follow the probable
opinion because it is more probable not only on the authority [of the moralists who support it], but still more for
the following reasons: the [contrary] law is not fully
enough known, and its weight is unbearable. Torni. Car.[?]
Burr.[?]. [p. 43]

As we can see, Pagano, Torni, and Sportelli, to whom we
might add Iorio, Fiorillo, Mazzini and other unidentified persons
(Car., Burr.), all formed a kind of friendly conspiracy to nudge
and reassure Alphonsus about probabilism. This was not without a certain mount of necessary exaggeration in order to get over
his obvious and painful reservations. These spiritual Fathers
would counsel and guide him for many years because, against
his own judgment, he would consult many and pray even more
before making any important decisions. But Pagano, his spiritual
director, kept telling him: "When your duty is unclear, your only
obligation is to do what seems right to you [*quel che ti piace*—
whatever you please]" (*Cose di coscienza*, pp. 20, 28b, 41, 51).

Was our Cartesian about to abandon reason and leap into the
void, held up only by the parachute of obedience? Yes and no.
No, when it came to directing others, as he was very well going
to show. Yes, when he was dealing with himself, for everyone
is as blind as Paul at Damascus until his sight is restored by
Ananias sent to him by the Risen Lord.[24] Pages 43 to 45 of the
Notebook of Conscience reasons precisely through this theology of obedience to one's director as God's own representative. Alphonsus invokes the authority of Saint Benedict, Saint
Bernard, and twice Saint Teresa of Ávila, his second mother
after Mary. Then he concludes:

Pagano, 1 January 1720—Rise above [doubts] and do what
is not an obvious evil without stopping, discussing or look-

ing for reasons; not to think about it, and act, with obedience as the only reason; at the first hesitation, go straight ahead without stopping. "Whoever listens to you listens to me."[25] "Go seek out Ananias." God wants thus to humble us. All [the theologians] agree, even if [the act prescribed by obedience] seems wrong to you. If you do the opposite, you are giving in to scruples. It is as though you were willingly getting drunk, at the risk of leaving your senses and making yourself good for nothing, etc.

If you do not wish to succumb to scruples, listen to your confessor who says "It is thus" when there is no certainty about the contrary. Is this not what the Psalms say[26] and what you yourself say to others?

This is how, after studying Genet, these men of great wisdom instead of Genet became Alphonsus' professors of probabilism. But this was a probabilism on command, not one of inner consent.

"These Poor Masses"

"The *infinite* malice of sin" was and is a theme for a sermon or a meditation. It has no place, even for a second, in the ministry of the confessional. André Malraux begins his *Antimemoires* with the following memory:

In 1940 I escaped with the future chaplain of the Vercors. We met again shortly afterward in the little town in the Drôme where he was parish priest....He had never been to Paris, having completed his studies at the seminary in Lyons. We talked far into the night, as friends do when they meet again, amid the homely village smells.

"How long have you been hearing confessions?"

"About fifteen years."

"What has confession taught you about men?"

"Oh, confession teaches nothing, you know, because when a priest goes into the confessional he becomes another person—grace and all that. And yet...first of all, people are much more unhappy than one thinks...and then...."

He raised his brawny lumberman's arms in the starlit night: "And then, the fundamental fact is that *there's no such thing as a grown-up person....*"[27]

The emphasis is Malraux's. He thought that this sentence was so filled with human truth that he let it set the tone of his book.

When he was still a young knight, Alphonsus already devoted himself to charity in the associations that took care of imprisoned priests, syphilitics in the chronic hospital of the *Incurabili,* men condemned to death and their orphaned families. These were miserable, but not evil, people. He felt that since Christ had come to save the lost sheep, he would have embraced them all.

Starting in January 1728 Alphonsus' confessional flooded with penitents from every class of society—in the end none of them were greater than the others. He left Naples in November 1732 to minister to forsaken country people. As he wrote to Benedict XIV, it was to come to "the aid of these poor masses" that he founded the Redemptorists; and it was to make them into good confessors that he wrote his *Moral Theologies.*

In constant touch with the poor and the suffering, he came to think of rigorism as a denial of the Gospel. Rigorism was a luxury reserved for theologians and wealthy, mature contemplatives, if there were any. Thus his association with and love for ordinary people taught him his moral theology. A harsh pastoral strategy affected him personally since it abused and cast into eternal despair those who were already the wretched of the earth, those whom he knew best because he was close to them and carried them in his heart like a mother carried her children. These were those for whom Christ came, the Christ whom he wanted to imitate.

It is significant that Alphonsus' first publication on ethics, as we shall see, would be to excuse from sin the rustics who curse the dead; for, he explained, "they know not what they do." Is this not one of the most surprising of Christ's sayings? And he taught it to us out of the depths of misery heaped upon him by human wickedness.

The poor were the best teachers of the moralist of mercy and hope for the hopeless. He gave himself to them so as to deny the predestination of the privileged elite alone; and, in turn, what he learned from the experience confirmed his conviction that "God...who desires everyone to be saved" (1 Tim 2:4). The poor were also the teachers of this moralist of sanctity. In the *Cappelle serotine* (evening chapels)[28] in the slums of Naples he marveled at the tenderness of love, the fervor, and the generosity that bloomed naturally in the hearts of the poor when they had the Gospel preached to them.

"THIRTY YEARS OF EXPERIENCE"

As we shall see, Alphonsus sharpened his pencils to write his first moral theology work in order for it to be read by his missionaries to the poor. Nor should it be forgotten that he was almost fifty years old. Up to this point, he had published only five slim pamphlets and three small books, among which, it is true, could be found his famous *Visits to the Blessed Sacrament*. Moreover, he was forced to write only out of continued dissatisfaction. The books he was always studying seemed to him either too exacting or too liberal for the people of God with whom he was so intimately in touch.

He knew a great deal about the dangers, vices, and the generosity of high society, having been totally steeped in it for twenty-six years, of which ten had been spent in litigation, with all its secret and crooked legal deals. Then for five years (1727–1732) he had been the most sought-after confessor in Naples, thronged by the nobles, the burgers, and the down-and-out masses of every estate and profession. Lastly, he had given his confessor's heart, strength, and ears for fifteen years to the poor in the countryside. The phrases "as I have learned by practice" and "experience proves that" frequently flow from his pen.

As the parachutist cannot fly away to the stars but must finally land on a square yard of ground, Alphonsus knew there could be no moral knowledge unless one floats down from high principles to solve life's problems on the ground in the here and now. He wrote: "The greatest difficulty in this line of knowledge is to apply principles rightly and in a new way to particular cases according to the many circumstances calling for different solutions."[29] Experience alone can claim to do this without presumption. In 1759, he wrote in the introduction to his *Homo Apostolicus,* a summary of the great *Moral Theology.*

> Taught on the one hand by reading theologians whom I studied while freeing myself from every passion, and enlightened on the other hand by thirty years of experience in confessions and missions, I composed my *Theologia Moralis.*[30]

In his great work he went even further, clearly tipping the scales on the side of experience: "I have set forth here many things that I learned in the exercise of missions and confessions, far more than from reading books."[31]

CHAPTER 3

FORTY YEARS
"IN THE MAKING"

In Alphonsus Liguori's long, intensely lived apostolate, he spent his time as a pastor, a founder, and a writer. The goal of all three activities was "to bring the Good News to the poor." What is intriguing is how the writer was able to publish more than a hundred and ten books and pamphlets, because he was not a writer by profession, like a prolific novelist whose livelihood depends on churning out two novels a year.[1] Most of Alphonsus' working life was devoted first to the stressful overwork of an urban ministry and then to the tasks of the missionary apostolate and the cares that occupied and preoccupied him as a superior general and a bishop.

His literary output cannot be explained in terms of a forty-hour workweek but of an eighty-hour one. The saint's terrible day included one hour for only one meal in the day and for recreation, five hours of sleep, eight hours of prayer, and ten hours of work; and, until at least 1762, most of this work consisted of a ministry that crushed lesser men.

Twenty-five percent of his writings are concerned with morality. The rest dealt with apologetics, dogmatics, liturgy, the ministry and, above all, spirituality.

He entered ethics by the back door. His doctrinal career[2] as a moralist began in 1746, when he was fifty years old, with a little study on cursing the dead that created quite a sensation. Ironically, the text is lost, but the repercussions which lasted until 1772 provide us with enough information to reconstruct it.[3]

"CURSING THE DEAD"

"Your ancestors be damned! Goddamn all of the dead!" The peasants of Pouille and elsewhere used to shout these pleasant words whenever they quarreled or accidentally hit their thumb with a hammer. This was seen as a grave mortal sin and a blasphemy for which some bishops reserved absolution to themselves alone.

Establishing himself at Deliceto at the end of 1744 and from there working in the regions of Foggia and Bari, Alphonsus did not take long to reject such severity. The importance given by some theoreticians to such language only served to multiply the number of sins weighing on the warped consciences of these little people who, without any great malice, did not think anything of cursing their animals, the wind, the rain, drought, or even the dead. For such a minor matter, they stayed away from the sacraments. Our missionary believed that these evil-sounding words really only helped people release their anger against a situation or a person, and did not express scorn or hatred for the souls in purgatory or the saints in heaven. His own experience provided him with the evidence.

In fact, for the extraordinary ministry of the mission, the bishops gave the priests the faculty to absolve sins normally reserved to the bishop. Many excommunicated individuals then took advantage of the mission to get themselves released. Alphonsus asked them whether they were actually thinking of the holy souls of the dead when they cursed, and the horrified response was always: "Father! Never! God forbid!" Alphonsus could not rest until he had set these blasphemers free and ended the evil practice that condemned them to hell. He therefore submitted a short memorandum to the three main diocesan missionary congregations in the capital—the *Illustrissimi* to which he belonged, the congregation of Father Pavone to which his friend G. Iorio belonged, and the missionary Congregation of Saint George—as well as to the Lazarists and the Pious Workers.[4] They unanimously responded that they already felt the same way or that they agreed with his arguments. In September 1746, he published the now lost *Letter in the Form of an Essay on the Abuse of Cursing the Dead*. It soon rallied much support, and in several dioceses this rather venial sin that could hardly be considered to be more than a mere reflex was stricken from the list of reserved cases. This was an appreciable victory of humanity and experience over principles as such.

But it was exactly on this major point that the moralist Alphonsus Liguori showed what he was capable of doing. A raging theologian writing under the pseudonym Cyriacus Chryseus ("the Golden Lord") quickly replied with a libelous pamphlet of nine caustic Latin columns. Since Alphonsus lived at Deliceto on the edge of an oak forest, the Golden Lord addressed him from the great height of his own knowledge: "Who are you to climb down from the trees to tell others what to do, as if you were a doctor of the law of God?" He further proceeded to crush him with his own version of faith and common sense:

Was the whole of antiquity deceived? So many churches deluded? So many philosophers, theologians, and bishops who understood nothing about this matter? Yet he alone claims to possess wisdom and understanding.

An avalanche of indisputable authorities was heaped upon
Alphonsus: Scripture, Tertullian, Saint Athanasius and Saint
Augustine, Saint Thomas and Cajetan, Duns Scotus and the
seventeenth-century Dominican Franceso Ghezzi, Plautus and
Juvenal—all of it sprinkled with Greek words.
Alphonsus felt he had to answer. He did so in an *Expiatio*
(explanation) which he published in 1748 as an appendix to his
Adnotationes in Busembaum (cols. 1029–32). He easily disposed of the reproach that he had not considered the views of
Augustine, Thomas Aquinas, Cajetan, and Duns Scotus, mainly
since these great teachers had never touched upon this local
Apulian problem. Moreover, he had not only consulted what
the Golden Lord called his "nondescript Congregation of country vagrants"—the Redemptorists—but had consulted each of
the five principal missionary congregations of Naples—"the
flower of the Neapolitan clergy"—who all agreed with him.

Was it in this way that I earned the glorious titles of ignorant, idiot, fool-hardy and so forth that my opponent be-
stows upon me? I turn the matter over to any man of sound
judgment.

Always on guard, the papal nuncio at Naples referred the
two documents to Benedict XIV. The pope asked Father
Tommaso Sergio of the Pious Workers (and a consultor to the
Holy Office) to examine them. Sergio pronounced in favor of
Liguori and returned the matter to the Holy Father. The pope,
after examining the writings personally, concurred.[5]
The conclusion: moral thought must shed light on life's "here
and now"—*hic et nunc*. Alphonsus found that the distant illumination from the biblical and patristic stars was not enough.

ADNOTATIONES IN BUSEMBAUM

The life of a tree can be explained in part by the chance conditions under which it has taken root and grown, whether the seed has been chosen and cared for in a nursery or cast by the wind into a rocky crevice. Literary works, like people, remain somewhat prisoners of their early childhood. This was never truer than for the *Theologia Moralis* by the founder of the Redemptorists.

Overwhelmed by the religious neglect of the rural poor, he founded his congregation in 1732. To give his Institute freedom to grow at the beginning, he felt it needed episcopal protection but not that of the local bishop. He thus placed himself under the direction of his friend Tommaso Falcoia, the former superior general of the Pious Workers, and bishop of Castellammare di Stabia since 1730. At the same time, Alphonsus declined to establish himself in Falcoia's diocese. Falcoia, still very much the superior general, wanted to govern everything, unfortunately. In particular he opposed Alphonsus' wish to admit young men into the congregation: he would accept only financially independent priests. Lacking papal approval, Alphonsus bent more or less to the dictates of a prelate he needed. Falcoia lived for another eleven years. Free at last in 1743, the founder immediately opened the Redemptorists' doors to eighteen-year-olds and organized studies for them at Ciorani and then at Deliceto after 1745. Because of the importance he attached to the administration of the sacrament of penance, especially during the missions, and also because of the confusion that reigned in moral theology, and even more because of his concern that his students—and the souls committed to their care—avoid the rigorist dead end that had stifled his own earlier years, he taught the moral theology courses himself when he was between missions.

His plan was rather humble. In 1756 he replied to an anonymous critic:

I certainly did not publish my *Theologia Moralis* to make a name for myself or to attract praise. I should indeed have been a fool if after having left the world and retired to a Congregation to bewail my sins, I then wasted so many years in weariness (for this work cost me ten years of excessive and extremely annoying weariness)....I had no other goal than to give glory to God and to help the young men of our Institute whose task is, nine months out of every year, to evangelize the neglected people in the countryside. For missionaries who spend most of their time hearing confessions, the most essential subject of study is moral theology. I wrote this work to set out for them briefly the most important ideas....And besides, I was unable to find any other moral theology book that I should have cared to put into their hands. The existing textbooks were in fact either too long or too short, too rigid or too lax.[6]

Unless he wanted to dictate his lectures—and he never allowed others to do it—he had to find an authoritative textbook. It had been a long time since he had spat out what the probabiliorist Genet poured down his throat in the seminary twenty years earlier. Instead he chose the book of a probabilist who came most closely to the ideal he was trying to reach. This was the *Medulla Theologiae Moralis* of the German Jesuit Hermann Busenbaum (1600–1668),[7] a volume of 655 small pages, clear and well organized, relatively short and yet thorough, of a kindly and moderate spirit. Published in Münster in 1650, it became the basic textbook preferred by the universities and seminaries that had resisted the rigorist tendencies of the second half of the seventeenth century. Between 1650 and 1770 it saw over two hundred editions. Busenbaum had become the received teaching in the probabilist school, and, although this school had become less well accepted in official circles, Alphonsus found himself more at home in it. Meekly but rigorously, he therefore undertook in the old tradition of the great teachers to write a commentary on the text. He enriched and corrected it, often adding long footnotes that nearly tripled its size. Believing his work would be useful to his colleagues and to other confessors, and aided by the generosity of his friend Giovanni Olivieri, he sent it to the printers.

On September 20, 1748, he wrote to Don Giuseppe Muscari, abbot of the monastery of San Basilio in Rome:

> My book has not come out yet….I think it is going to be useful. In a relatively limited space, it deals with the most essential questions in Moral Theology, especially those related to practice….
>
> It has cost me years and years of weariness, in particular almost the entire last five years [1744–1748] with eight, nine, and ten hours of work a day. It horrifies me just thinking of it.[8]

The words "in particular almost the entire last five years" indicate that before 1743 some major components of the work had at least been sketched out. At Rome we possess a copy of the ninth edition of Busenbaum's *Medulla Theologiae Moralis* published in 1733 in Padua and annotated by Alphonsus himself. That was in Year One of his Congregation. Imitating the Neapolitan academies that gave a continuing high quality education, the missionaries held three meetings a week: one on the pastoral ministry of the missions, one on a point of dogma, and one on a moral case. The topics were posted in advance so that everyone could study it in advance and come to the meeting well prepared. Tannoia wrote:

> In 1748, at the insistence of his colleagues, Alphonsus had made copious notes on Bussembau [sic] and gave a copy of this work to Giuseppe Nicolai, the archbishop of Conza. His notes contained all sorts of moral cases solved on the missions. His spiritual sons urged him to publish it so that they could have them.[9]

The book thus had a double origin: to solve concrete cases encountered by the missionaries among the country poor, and to educate young men for this kind of ministry. The first stage of the work consisted of research and scattered notes based on the moral cases seen year after year in the field. The second stage was five years' intense activity (1744–1748) spent in annotating the whole of the students' future textbook. Alphonsus used a copy of the *Medulla* (1737) now preserved at Catanzaro for the structure of his *Adnotationes in Busembaum*.[10]

Alphonsus' was not the first commentary on the German Jesuit. Claude Lacroix (1652–1714) devoted eight volumes to him in what was one of the great works of eighteenth-century moral theology published between 1707–1714. A hundred and forty years later another commentary, by the Jesuit Antonio Ballerini (1805–1881) was published posthumously in seven volumes (1889–1893). Ballerini was the sworn enemy of Saint Alphonsus and was only defeated when Alphonsus was proclaimed a Doctor of the Church. His work was completed and published by Father Domenico Palmieri. Either of these great teachers would have sufficed to immortalize Busenbaum. They certainly justify Alphonsus' choice of Busenbaum as a basic textbook. Still, it was Alphonsus, placed chronologically between the other two commentators, who in fact brought the most honor to the work and the name of the German Jesuit. The volume appeared in Latin, naturally, at the end of 1748 with the title: *R.P.D. Alphonsi de Ligorio adnotationes in Busembaum* on the fly-leaf and on the title page, *Medulla Theologiae Moralis R.P. Hermanni Busembaum, s.j., cum adnotationibus per R.P.D. Alphonsum de Ligorio, Rectorem majorem Congregationis SS. Salvatoris...ad usum juvenum praefatae Congregationis...Expensis D. Joannis Olivieri.*[11] The longer the title, the humbler and more precise the work. The short preface underlines both:

For several years I looked for a book which would satisfy the need to instruct novices of our Congregation as briefly and methodically as possible in *Moral Theology*, a difficult subject necessary in the work of saving souls. I read, reread, and examined many authors; but it seemed to me that some were too exhaustive while others were too succinct. From among them all, I chose Busembaum. Organized, concise and complete, he provided the essential baggage. Yet I also felt it was my duty to develop a certain point or complete another, on the authority of well-known teachers, viz., Saint Thomas, Lessius, Sanchez, Castro Palao, Lugo, Layman, Bonacina, Viva, Lacroix, Roncaglia, etc., and above all the Doctors of Salamanca.... You will find here in brief very nearly everything that they treat at length, especially practical matters.

Therefore, we should not look to the *Adnotationes* for a moral system. The author is concerned with resolving cases of conscience. This he did, guided by intrinsic principles clarified by Christian wisdom and an already lengthy experience. He was fifty-two years old.

THE GROWTH OF THE *THEOLOGIA MORALIS*

The *Adnotationes* [Tannoia writes] were enthusiastically greeted by the [ecclesiastical] public. It was Alphonsus who quickly became dissatisfied. He thought that the explanations were insufficiently supported (*non munita di sufficiente criterio*). Thus he republished the work expanded into two thick volumes and dedicated to Benedict XIV.[12]

The second edition retained Busenbaum's basic structure but, owing to its changes and its length, it was in fact a new book. As its title claimed, it was indeed a *Moral Theology Compiled by Rev. Fr. Alphonsus Liguori*: a *Theologia Moralis concinnata a R.P.D. Alfonso de Ligorio...per appendices in Medullam R.P.H. Busembaum.* The author explained himself in a new preface:

For many years I had wanted to provide the young men of our missionary Society who are called to enlighten consciences through instruction and confession with a book of moral theology that would maintain a just mean between excessive severity and overindulgence. I did it. Other people were satisfied with the work, but I was not. There was too much of a rush to get it published. Some points were not sufficiently worked out, while others were not well organized....I therefore set to work on a second edition...that I have expanded with some very useful questions. All things considered, I have also retracted certain opinions. After all, I am only human. I am not ashamed to change my mind. Saint Augustine and Saint Thomas did the same.[13]

In fact, he corrected fifty-eight opinions in the first volume, published in 1753 and forty-one in the second, published after a two-year interval in 1755. After the appearance of the first, he wrote to his spiritual sons, the Redemptorists, on August 8, 1754:

> Be miserly with time. Use it to pray and to visit the Blessed Sacrament (He is there precisely to welcome our visits). Use it to study, for study is absolutely necessary for our purpose.
>
> In this regard, I recommend that confessors study Moral Theology and that they do not blindly follow certain opinions of the doctors without having weighed their intrinsic reasons. I speak in particular of those opinions that in my second edition I no longer acknowledge as probable. Along with the probabilists, I say that every confessor is obliged to act as follows: for each question, he must find out whether there is an intrinsic reason that is capable of convincing the mind; for thus is the contrary opinion rendered improbable. If a convincing reason is missing, we can then, and only then, rely on extrinsic probability. But be careful here, for I fear that many in our Congregation may have quite deceived themselves on this point. And note well that in this second edition, I usually admit as probable only those opinions that I have labeled as such. I do not claim that everyone ought to adopt my views, but I beg you to be so good as to read my book and consider what I have written at the cost of so much work, research, and study before rejecting it. For, my brothers, I did not write this work for the general public or for fame. Were I to gain only the passing smoke of vainglory, I would have willingly spared myself this labor; God knows what it has cost me in trouble and weariness. I wrote it solely for you,

my brothers, so that we ourselves might adhere to a sure
doctrine and at least that we think before we act. I confess
to you that many opinions that at first I took seriously I
have subsequently recognized as improbable. I beg all of
you, young men and confessors, to read my work because
I have written it for you. You may all act afterwards as
you believe you should before God.[14]

Benedict XIV conveyed the following message of thanks to
Alphonsus for the *Moral Theology* dedication: "You can be sure
that it will have a great success everywhere and that its authority will be recognized." The papal secretaries sent equally generous words of praise to the Dominican Daniele Concina (1687–
1756) whom Alphonsus Liguori opposed as *severissimo* (most
strict) but whom Benedict XIV definitely favored. Such are the
subtleties of government, where the right hand does not know
what the left is writing. Of greater worth is another testimony
that Tannoia also reports about Alphonsus:

Brother Tommaso Cherubino, the shining light of today's
Dominicans and a professor at the Royal University of
Naples rightly said that the eminent author of the *Theologia
Moralis* possesses the wonderful art of skirting the reefs
of both laxism and rigorism where the majority of other
teachers come to grief.[15]

Nevertheless, Alphonsus' work would end up commanding
the great pope's attention and his esteem. Benedict XIV's *De
Synodo diocesana* would refer to Alphonsus as *prudens auc-
tor*—a learned, prudent, judicious, and wise author.[16] Ques-
tioned about a case by G. Iorio, he answered: "You have your
Liguori. Ask his advice."[17]

With the appearance of the second volume in the spring of

1755, Alphonsus' major work was there for all to see. He was now almost sixty years old, but his work on this book was not yet finished. For all of his other books he made three corrections—once on the manuscript, the second on the galley proofs, and the third on the first edition. He never touched them again after the second edition was published. But even after the second edition was published, he continued to think and to work on his *Moral Theology* until the eighth edition of 1779. He lived with an essentially unfinished manuscript for thirty-one years and invested it with second thoughts, adaptations, refinements, additions, and complementary essays in a constant effort to keep it a faithful reflection of his thinking about familiar and new problems. The manuscript became the repository for all of his discussions, his consultations, his experience, and his reading. He also wrote and rewrote the book while trying to remain within the divine illumination, for he never studied or wrote without gazing at and directing his prayers to the crucified Christ and Our Lady of Good Counsel whose pictures were on his desk. In 1762 he wrote: "It has almost been forty years that I have been studying moral theology, and I am always finding something new." And "Moral theology is an endless black hole. I never stop reading and I never stop finding new things. I note down the most important."[18]

He did not work alone, however. One would like to know more about the intellectual and missionary climate around 1750 that was created by the presence of Giovanni Mazzini, Girolamo Ferrara, Alessandro Di Meo and, shortly afterward, Gaspare Caione, priests who were, respectively, a theologian, a Latinist, a historian, and a lawyer. And then there were the students, led by their prefect Muscari. Nor would it be right to overlook the young priest Aniello Ruscigno, who died in 1755 at the age of thirty-two, exhausted in reading sources, looking up references, making indexes, and correcting proofs. Meanwhile Alphonsus carefully considered all of the material and wrote almost everything in his own hand: there are 1,474 pages containing more than 70,000 statements from more than 800 authors.[19] Three years later Father Pasquale Amendolara, a victim also of exhaustion over the third and fourth editions of the *Theologia Moralis* (1757, 1760) and only thirty-five years old, joined Ruscigno in the cemetery at Pagani.

During the twenty-year period between 1749 to 1769, nine *Dissertations*, *Ripostes*, or *Apologies* appeared to correct or supplement the first six editions. All of them dealt with the use of probable opinion in moral theology. Alphonsus was seeking out, establishing, and then defending his moral system. We shall return to this later.

But first we must see how the tree that is the *Theologia Moralis* grew and spread its branches. Starting with the second edition (1755), the author added his *Pratica del Confessore* in Italian. This contained his pastoral teaching on sin, the Christian life, holiness, and mysticism. "Without this," he wrote to his Venetian publisher Giuseppe Remondini, "my *Moralia* would be truncated and incomplete."[20]

His *Moralia* spread throughout Europe, with the Italian *Practica*. But that was not good enough! Translated into Latin by himself and by Fathers Caione and Ferrara under his direction, the *Praxis Confessarii* was incorporated into the third edition (3 volumes, 1757) and in all the succeeding ones—nine editions during the author's lifetime and seventy-three after his death.

But three folio volumes were expensive and long to read—in Latin at that! Alphonsus thought of the poor—the empty wallets and the priests who had forgotten their Latin. In the same year and after prodigious work he wrote a summary in Italian of his large and pastoral *Moralia* with the title *Istruzione e Pratica per un Confessore*.

And the same thing happened all over again. People outside Italy wanted these three small octavo summary volumes. Remondini pleaded with Alphonsus to translate them into Latin. *Homo Apostolicus* thus appeared in 1759. Entirely free of Busenbaum and entirely reworked, this book is without doubt the most personal, the most mature, and the most finished of all of Alphonsus' books as a moral theologian. It would go through one hundred and eighteen editions.

But over and above the poor, Alphonsus was thinking of the poorest of the poor. He simplified and further summarized the *Istruzione e Pratica* (*Homo Apostolicus*) in a volume published in 1764 with the title *Il Confessore diretto per le Confessioni della Gente di Campagna*. He wrote to Remondini on August 26, 1763:

> I have made an abridged version in the vernacular with enough of the details of all of the main points in moral theology. My booklet is short, but he who possesses it is perfectly capable of hearing confessions in the villages. And it is with this goal that I have written it for use in my diocese.[21]

Alphonsus Liguori had been bishop of Sant'Agata dei Goti—Saint Agatha of the Goths—for the previous two years. The crozier, however, did not replace the pen.

CHAPTER 4

SOURCES AND METHODS

Is it possible to find in Scripture, the Councils, and the Holy Fathers the authorities for resolving every case of conscience that may arise?

As anyone can easily ascertain by reading my work, there does not exist a single case the solution of which cannot be deduced from the principles drawn from Scripture, the Councils, and the Fathers.

How is it, then, that some authors have pursued new opinions? Laxist opinions?

This blindness is chiefly the result of the boldness with which some have dared to resolve for themselves very difficult questions by trusting in their own judgment....For the blindness of the human mind in moral matters is all the greater as our will, inclined towards evil after the Fall of Adam, greatly deepens the darkness which clouds our understanding. That is why whoever relies solely upon human reason will have great difficulty to avoid falling into error.[1]

This is François Genet talking to his reader. Such is the speech of a theologian replying from his ivory tower to the casuist grubbing about in the muck and rubble of the moat below.

BETWEEN THEOLOGIANS AND CASUISTS— A MORAL THEOLOGIAN

In a magisterial lecture at the National Meeting of University Chaplains in Strasbourg, April 4–6, 1984, the Dominican Father Jean-Pierre Lintanf told the following anecdote:

At the invitation of Cardinal Renaud a research committee on ethics was established at Lyons. Ten theologians worked for two years, and we brought out a short text on the Church's position on ethical questions. Now, in this text was the following sentence: "We cannot extract from the gospels a moral system in the sense of a coherent list of precepts and norms that would allow us immediately to rule our personal and social conduct." Everyone was in agreement when, from the other end of the room, the cardinal interrupted me while I was reading the text and said, "But, Father, you are not going to have me believe that there are no exact, easily understood, easily applied, well-known precepts in the Gospels!" I replied, "Yes, of course, there are. For example, to call no one 'father'!"

Jesus gave principles and pointed presumably intelligent people in the right direction, but he refrained from solving concrete cases. He said: "If someone strikes you on the right cheek, turn to him the left." But when he himself was struck in the presence of the high priest, he did not turn the other cheek. He demanded an explanation: "Why do you strike me?" A new situation required a new solution. A solution in the spirit of the Gospels but dictated by circumstances.

Here, in a word, is the reason for the morass of moral theology debates during the seventeenth and eighteenth centuries among the self-styled moralists. The rigorists harked back to the ancient and pure sources. They therefore could spend their entire lives doing nothing but scrutinizing the Scriptures and the Fathers. Genet's title shows it: *Theologia Moralis, seu Resolutiones casuum conscientiae juxta Sacrae Scripturae, Canonum et Sanctorum Patrum mentem.* In fact, he very often quotes the Holy Fathers, but according to a selective principle keeping only the most severe, while he shies from quoting anyone later than the sixteenth century. The laxists, however, were content with plucking the most liberal opinions from the most recent authors if only they had the slightest shadow of probability. Between the two extremes, moralists declined either to separate themselves from a world full of innovation or to get joyfully bogged down in it. Was there no way of reconciling morality and modern life? Many thought that there was—on the condition of holding on to the light of the Scriptures and the Fathers in those areas they had illuminated while, *at the same time,* relying on reason and recent teachers for any new problems.

This was certainly the road Alphonsus followed in reaction to Genet. The rigorists did not forgive him for quoting only recent authors, aside from Saint Thomas. Indeed, he was content with the moralists who wrote after the Council of Trent.[2] Aware that renewal was necessary, he wrote:

The office of confessor is the greatest—it concerns eternal salvation—and the most difficult. The most difficult because it requires knowledge of all the sciences, all work, all the professions; because it touches upon every kind of problem; because it presupposes knowledge of a huge number of positive laws and sacred canons that have to be rightly interpreted and, finally, because *there remains the hard work of applying all of this to the diversity of cases for which circumstances call for different solutions.*

Some pride themselves on being scholars and distinguished theologians and disdain to read the moralists whom they scornfully call casuists. It is enough, they say, for the confessor to know general principles of morality to solve every particular case.

It is certainly true that all particular cases are to be solved in the light of principles. But the whole difficulty consists exactly in applying to particular cases obscured by complex circumstances the general principles appropriate to them. Reason comes into play in order to weigh the pros and cons of each principle. This is the task performed by the moralists.[3]

And Alphonsus comments ironically with a backward glance at his seminary textbook:

Our opponents cry: Let the books of the casuists be gathered together and cast into the fire, and let only the books of the Holy Scriptures, the councils, the holy canons, and the Holy Fathers be read!...It would please God that we find the solutions to cases of conscience in them! Now, the Scriptures themselves present many questions, the Fathers stand in need of commentators, and, as Vincent of Lerins says, they are not authoritative in the details of the divine *law* but when they are *unanimous* about a point of *faith*.[4]

Fifteen years later, in 1764, after still more experience in reading so many authors whose different views used the same Gospel text or the Fathers, he returned to the subject in his *Response to a Letter from a Religious on the Use of Equally Probable Opinion*:

58

You write that "we must follow the Scriptures, the councils, the canons and the Holy Fathers." Very well! But, Father, God grant that we find in the Scriptures the solutions to all the moral problems! No one doubts that what the Scriptures say is to be preferred to the pronouncements of all the authors! But when? When they are clear and not when they are used in a partisan way by certain people who would make them say what they do not say. I will spare you those numerous passages from the Holy Books that our opponents throw against us in order to make us admit that it is illicit to follow a probable opinion; but the exegetes give these passages a completely different meaning. As for the councils, canons, and Holy Fathers, I say as much again: if only they could relieve all our moral doubts! They had other purposes than to solve cases of conscience: they devoted themselves to fixing the dogmas of faith. As for those rare points that they taught concerning morals, we receive them with veneration and obedience. Our opponents pile up texts from the Fathers in order to forbid the use of probable opinion; but our authors have no difficulty in making a good show of the many texts which say the contrary....

For the rest, which Fathers have written treatises on restitution, contracts, sales, taxes, loans, associations, ecclesiastical benefices, simony, censorship, fasting and other such things?

We can recognize the lawyer behind this list. And even if these particular questions are not our spiritual questions, the problems are the same, multiplied a hundredfold. Alphonsus had thus all the more reason to tease the ivory-tower theologians. He continues:

A certain author, a fashionable probabiliorist and theologian to the bishop of Soissons, writes that in morality one must follow the rule of the Divine Scriptures interpreted according to the unanimous consent of the Fathers. All very well! But who has all of the writings of the Fathers nearby and the time to go through them to find them all agreeing on the meaning of the inspired text that will clear up his doubt?[5]

To take a rather obvious example: in Scripture illuminated by the unanimity of the Fathers, what criteria will we find concerning a just war? Are they the same in the era of the crossbow (in the eleventh century), the musket (in the seventeenth century), and of nuclear weapons?

Certainly, the highest rule for humanity is the will of God. Revelation and Natural Law help us to discover it. Take the Sabbath law for instance. But, how do we apply it? The Pharisees absolutized the law; man is made for the Sabbath. Jesus absolutized persons; the Sabbath is made for man. Alphonsus writes: "The remote, material rule of our action is the divine law; its proximate, formal rule is really conscience...which is the practical decision of reason."[6] But reason is not infallible. It can be mistaken. "When it is invincibly [unconscious of being] mistaken, it does not sin. Better—it probably acquires some merit."[7] Might we ask whether reason could make a mistake about the Natural Law without committing a mortal sin and damning itself? Alphonsus replies: "Then damn, if you dare, Saint Thomas and Saint Bonaventure, who contradicted each other on points of Natural Law and died without retracting their views!"[8]

He would not use any doctrinal system, even if the latter began with scriptural Revelation or Natural Law, to solve life's concrete moral problems. He would use a different method, one that would be evangelical, rational, and wise.

THE ALPHONSIAN METHOD

It is essential to distinguish Alphonsus' *method*, which was already present in his first commentaries on Busenbaum, from his *moral system*, which grew out of his method and would continue to grow until 1762.

What, then, is Alphonsus' method?

First, he refused to read only those New Testament texts that frightened mainly because they had been badly interpreted: "Many are called, but few are chosen"; "Strait is the way, and the gate also, and few who pass through it." He also meditated on the parables of mercy such as "I am come for the lost"; "God wants all people to be saved"; "Ask and you shall receive."

Then, before God, he weighed the pros and cons of a case, leaving aside the authorities, unless they had something helpful to say, until he reached a conclusion. Tannoia writes:

Alphonsus did not belong to any school. He respected them all, but he respected reason more while giving absolute respect to the Church's decisions. He often censured as too lenient the judgments of the most rigid theologians; while just as often, he objected to those of the easy-going theologians as too harsh. He explains himself in his dedicatory letter to Benedict XIV: "Over the years, I have read a mass of theologians—some of tolerant opinion, others of rigid—but I found the former too indulgent and the latter too severe. From that time I believed that there was a useful work to be attempted—that of publishing a text which would keep to the just mean and in which I would give those opinions closest to the truth and most important to know."

...He willingly said: "Where neither the canons nor the

Gospel provide a clear indication it is up to reason to guide us. If reason cannot lead me out of the darkness, I cannot go ahead blindly, but must leave it to others to guide my reason." To clear up a case, he had recourse to prayer and spent months examining various opinions. If his doubt persisted, not content with consulting his colleagues, he sought counsel from Rome, from Naples, and from the most highly reputed theologians.[9]

This was not to count the opinions pro and con and to decide in favor of the majority, but rather to weigh the merits of the reasons upon which they were based. He explains his position in a solemn declaration in which both the man of God and the man of the Enlightenment appear in their full stature:

It may occur rather often in this *Theologia Moralis* that I do not please everyone. The ardent partisans of rigorism or of leniency will find me either too severe or too indulgent. Too severe because I have often set myself at a distance from numerous and weighty authors. Too indulgent because I have approved opinions favorable to human freedom.

Alphonsus had run up his colors. In the scientific spirit of his time, he challenged arguments based on authority. On his scales, the great authors in morality were weighty neither by their status nor by their number, but by their arguments. Alphonsus professed the following:

With God as my witness, whose honor alone and the salvation of souls matters to me, I have written nothing out of passion, nor to conform myself to the views of this or that author, nor from a leaning towards rigorism or laxism.

On every question, after having studied it a long time, I strove to determine the truth, especially on those chiefly involving conduct.

Thus he had studied the ancients (of the sixteenth and seventeenth centuries) and his contemporaries and

weighed their reasons on an exact scale, sometimes spending many days in coming to a decision. For I did not, like a sheep, blindly follow an author but sought to reach the truth or, at least, to come as close to it as possible. As much as possible, I strove to have reason come before authority; and where their reasons failed to convince me, I did not hesitate to contradict many authors.

"To reach the truth," "to attain to the truth"—we can clearly see his goal. But is he really that different from any other authors with their a priori reasons and authorities? One could hardly fail to protest to Alphonsus: "Nevertheless, you still chiefly quote from the partisans of a tolerant morality." And he would respond:

I did not omit to read the rigorists, ready to change my mind if their reasons convinced me of their truth. But instead of reasons, very often they felt only the need of arrogance or of irony in order to claim to be right. How would I have been able to follow in all things people who claimed that their reasons were in greater conformity to the truth or the Gospel by the sole fact that they were the most rigid? And who often rejected contrary opinions as false and opposed to the Gospel by the sole fact that they were favorable to human freedom?
Besides...as the Doctors agree in teaching and as the

learned Father Concina (although a celebrated exponent of rigid doctrines) informs me, we must impose on men nothing on pain of grave sin unless the reason for doing so is quite clear....

Finally, given the weakness of human nature, it is not true for souls that the narrowest way is always the surest.[10]

Quoting Saint Antoninus, Alphonsus states elsewhere:

Those who oblige others to follow opinions that are too rigid are working for the powers of Hell. They are the cause of the damnation of those they have convinced of these opinions and who are lost by not being able to follow them [since even an erroneous conscience is always binding]. As Saint John Chrysostom advises: Be austere in your own conduct, be indulgent towards that of others.[11]

Everything that is good to do is not always good to prescribe. With his claim to discover truth by reason rather than through authority, did Alphonsus think that he was infallible? Far from it! He continued his solemn declaration in the following words:

I vow that if any error has escaped my notice, I hope that it will be pointed out to me. I am ready to retract it immediately and shamelessly. Nor was I ashamed in this second edition to reject a goodly number of opinions that I had judged probable and that later appeared to me to be either too wide or too narrow.[12]

In fact, he had prepared a list of ninety-nine propositions from his *Adnotationes* which he believed ought to be revised.

In the sixth edition of 1767, he retracted twenty-three more, and three more again in the eighth and penultimate edition of 1779. Aside from fifteen in which he judged himself too severe, all the other second thoughts were revisions in the direction of greater severity.

It is hard not to see here a probabilist "under orders" to advance but who is slowly forced to retreat to what came to be known equiprobabilism.

Of course, he was chided by his friends and spiritual sons:

"Father, if you contradict yourself like this, you will compromise your reputation and the success of your books!"
"Let them say of me what they will. I am not seeking my own glory, but the good of souls and the glory of Jesus Christ."[13]

An impassioned search for truth! But which truth? Here we find the second element in the Alphonsian method. It is a search not for a theoretical truth for knowledge's sake, but for a practical truth in order to act. Just as doctrinal or dogmatic theology resembles the theoretical nature of the pure sciences, moral theology resembles the applied sciences. In the science of right acts, clear-sightedness does not depend only upon one's own sharp eyes and height, but rather more upon the particularities of the people and situations one is trying to see. It depends on experience as well, and on what is actually possible and best. In this realm, virtue is more necessary than knowledge. And the cardinal virtue here is called prudence.

Prudence—that is, the perpetual discovery, beyond the most rigorous but atemporal speculation, of a true and just conduct in the singular circumstances of the moment. It goes much further than the theory which *speaks the truth*; it is the exalted practical wisdom that *does the truth* in a particular action.[14]

In *The Degrees of Knowledge*, Jacques Maritain explains that the mystical theology of Saint John of the Cross was "practically practical," the fruit of a personal experience of prudence. He then adds:

Analogous remarks should suitably be made about that very great practical, as well as speculative, moralist, Saint Alphonsus Liguori. The teaching of these saints is, to our mind, a much purer example of practically practical moral science than are certain works on casuistry, which can be reproached for being too speculative in mode and tending to misunderstand the absolutely irreducible role of the virtue of prudence in the proper regulation of human acts— a virtue which no science could ever replace, because only prudence can judge infallibly of the contingent itself.[15]

Which is to say, there are unforeseen complexities which fill life but which, each one, come only once.

Benedetto Croce (d. 1952), who was quite familiar with the Neapolitan eighteenth century, even the religious side of it, once said to Father Domenico Capone:

Alphonsus de Liguori was no casuist. He wasn't because even in setting out the rules for solving cases, he let himself be guided not by abstract schemes, but by an intuition of reality.[16]

This is the intuition which Bergson distinguishes so aptly from speculative intelligence. "Intelligence," he said, "is inadequate for understanding life; only intuition suffices." Intuition, Bergson says, is the direct grasping, the immediate vision, a "sympathy" with the object, which here is life. Knowing something of life is the first step in moral theology.

CHAPTER 5

ALPHONSUS'
MORAL SYSTEM

The method of prudence is usually sufficient to enlighten the conscience directly; nevertheless, it does not succeed in solving all problems: rights and duties remain in doubt. Conscience is thus like a court of law in which two litigants—freedom and the law—contend. Let us understand law in the wider sense of obligation, of the will of God. Lacking a direct way, conscience escapes from indecision by an indirect path, a reflex principle. Reflex principles differ according to the moral system to which the moralist refers.

The phenomenon of moral systems appeared during the sixteenth century to face the complexity of a new world whose problems agonized consciences and divided scholars.

While his method of merciful prudence, inspired by the Gospel and the result of personal holiness, had been present almost at the beginning of his ministry, for a long time Alphonsus sought his own moral system. He only began to articulate it at the age of sixty-six in 1762 in his *Breve dissertazione dell'uso moderato dell'opinione probabile* (*A Brief Dissertation of the Moderate Use of Probable Opinion*), printed at Naples in 1762, published later in Latin as an appendix to *Confessore diretto* (1764), and inserted into the sixth edition of the *Theologia Moralis* (1767).

THIRTY YEARS OF RESEARCH

Bitterly opposed by both rigorists and laxists, Alphonsus would write dissertations, apologias and notes to develop and then defend his system. From the time of his death until the middle of the twentieth century, whole forests were depleted to supply paper for books and articles that would continue the debate and not always objectively.[1] The fury surrounding Alphonsus' system, by both parties trying to claim Alphonsus as their own, is equaled only by the utter indifference into which the whole question has fallen today.

Nonetheless, Father Liguori's intellectual travels and the stands he took in defining his moral system deeply affected his private life and the public life of the founder of the Redemptorists. We know where he began. As an impressionable seminarian and knight for the glory of God, he was nurtured on probabiliorism and showed himself to be an ardent rigorist. Still, he put so much of his heart, zeal, prayers, and personal penances into "working over" hardened sinners and backsliders that he was able never to refuse an absolution.

But he realized that the rigorism taught by the ivory-tower intellectuals was not applied in the field by the most important missioners, that it was theoretically weak and practically harmful. After authoritative advice, therefore, he changed sides to probabilism.

He did not change his allegiance immediately. For this sensitive soul, it was made at the price of the most painful crisis of conscience. As we have seen, some of the pages of his private notes reveal a long conflict. But his successive directors—Pagano, Falcoia, Cafaro—and his advisers and coworkers—Torni, Iorio, Villani, Muscari—in a way drove him to this position, one proven by his personal experience and reassuringly adopted under obedience.

To cite merely the most important texts by their content and their date, on page 227 of his second notebook we can make out these tormented sentences (emphasis by Alphonsus):

> *Special obediences*—24 October 1741, Monsignor Falcoia told me to avail myself of the probable opinion, as so many others do. Moreover, Dom Paolo [Cafaro] ordered me to stop worrying or tormenting myself over it. *I vowed to carry out this obedience, today 13 July 1748.*

Some years later he adds: "Moreover, if I am troubled by scruples during confessions, Dom Paolo told me to drive them away like a temptation. See Muscari p. 233. Same advice from Villani."

What exactly do Muscari and the others say on page 233? The following extract shows how Alphonsus' sensitive conscience had become a playing field where the probable opinion always won:

> Muscari. I am obliged to obey, even if the confessor is a probabilist. It is at least more probable that I am thus bound. The contrary is a temptation. Thus to be driven away is a temptation. Andrea Villani and Paolo Cafaro say the same. 18 September 1751—Moreover, [Muscari says] I am bound by obedience—when in doubt, it is obedience that prevails—and by my vow, to follow the probable opinion by the reflex motive that our opinion is at least more probable by virtue of this *great preponderance* which suffices to make it sure and certain.[2]

Even though these quotations are somewhat cryptic, they provide evidence that if Alphonsus affirmed the principles of probabilism for nearly thirty years, it was in part by will and obedience, *without his having arrived at a tranquil and assured personal conviction.* As a confessor, as one responsible for a Congregation of missionaries, and as a teacher of moral theology, he chose, commented on, and reedited the best probabilist of the age (1748) and shortly thereafter (1749) he took the time and the pains to persuade himself—without complete success—and to persuade others of the probabilist system. His spiritual director and his confidants leaned on the scales and gave probabilism the weight necessary to tip them sufficiently to convince Alphonsus. He thus published a rigorous Latin *Dissertation* on the question: can one follow a probable opinion against a more probable opinion? He replied: *"Constat"*—"Certainly." This for two reasons:

    I. "Whoever has a probable opinion in his favor acts with prudence."

    II. A law binds only if it is certain. "When the law is doubtful, freedom holds," that is, it takes precedence.

Some scholars have wished to downplay the importance of this 1749 *Dissertation.* It was only an anonymous essay and never published in the strict sense of the word.[3] If one looks at the last page (47) of the original edition, however, one sees that the printer Pellechia and the editor Savastano both actually name Alphonsus Liguori in their request to Monsignor Torni for permission to print the essay. The Jesuit Francesco Antonio Zaccaria, a friend and colleague of Alphonsus, writes in his *Storia letteraria* (VI, 1754), that the pamphlet contributed to the author's theological fame.[4] Alphonsus' little work ended with a missionary appeal to young moralists: "Do not enter the confessional without having carefully read our [probabilist] authors. Only afterwards, choose between rigor and gentleness."

And he adds the following lines which reflect his own battle for inner peace in the spirit of Christ:

It is our joy to think that we shall be summoned not before the tribunal of the probabiliorists, but before that of Christ who condemns only the transgressions of the laws of which we have certain knowledge.

The following *Dissertation* of 1755 resumes almost exactly the same doctrine and arguments—with the important difference that Alphonsus sets himself up more as an adversary of probabiliorism than as a partisan of probabilism.

The success of his *Moral Theology* was such that scarcely had volume II of the Neapolitan edition appeared in 1755 than Alphonsus was negotiating with the great Venetian publisher Giuseppe Remondini to bring out a third edition. On February 15, 1756, he wrote to him:

I repeat to you my recommendation: Do not entrust the examination of my book to some theologian who adheres to the rigid opinion (as do most Dominicans today), for I am not at all of this opinion but hold to the just mean. A Jesuit would be preferable, as these Fathers are truly masters in the science of Moral Theology. What is certain is that the Jesuits of Naples went so far as to praise my work publicly. Some of them only said that I showed myself rather rigid on certain points. But let me repeat: I wanted to keep to the just mean.[5]

While at Naples preaching to the clergy, he wrote again:

You have only received the first volume at present. Print it in whatever format pleases you. Meanwhile, I shall set about preparing the second, for I have important additions to make that I have borrowed in large part from the recently published [moralist] Lacroix, edited by Father Zaccaria. You tell me that you will entrust the examination to a Jesuit Father. This pleases me greatly, for if it were a Dominican, he would follow, as does his Order today, the teaching of Father Concina and would object to a number of opinions I have accepted as being too broad. In fact, I have usually followed the direction of the Jesuits rather than that of the Dominicans, for the opinions of the Jesuits are neither too broad nor too rigid but maintain the just mean. And if I uphold some rigid opinion against one Jesuit writer or another, I almost always do so by relying upon the authority of other writers of the Society. Besides, I admit that it is from them that I have learned what little I have put into my books. This is in fact because (and I do not stop repeating it), where Moral Theology is concerned, they have been and are masters....Thus I am guided in my decisions by what my conscience dictates to me as the most just....Therefore, be well convinced that I am neither very rigid nor very broad.

I beg of you to let the examiner read the present letter in order that he may know what system that I have embraced. I am following now as in the present book, not the system of probabiliorism or rigorism, but that of probabilism.[6]

Ten days after this letter, on April 8, 1756, Alphonsus returned to Pagani. Scarcely arrived, he was taken with fever and violent headaches. Soon he was much more ill. From the eve of Palm Sunday until Holy Saturday (April 10–12), his life hung by a thread. We can hear him repeating: "Oh, what a grace it would be to die during Holy Week!"

He gave Father Villani, who was founding a new house at St. Angelo at Cupolo, the interim government of the Institute should he die. A letter was given to him from the Sisters of Scala: "I shall acknowledge it on the Day of Judgment." He confided to the attendant: "My *Theologia Moralis* is finished. During Holy Week I shall escape from this world!" The attendant urged him: "Begin another work and live a little longer." But Alphonsus quickly replied: "That's good! Live longer and sin!" Later, a priest said to him: "On every side they are praying for your recovery." Alphonsus harrumphed: "They would do better to pray that the Lord make me a Saint and that I die in his grace."

He got better, but the young priest Giuseppe Melchionna, who wrote down these sayings, also preserved the following great revelation:

I have no worries. *Only one thing bothers me: it is to have followed the probable opinion.* But I did it under my director's orders and I vowed to follow it. Should I reproach myself on this matter? To sin one must have the will to sin. I do not want to sin at all; and of that, I am morally certain. The Lord, I am sure, has forgiven the past.[7]

A secret dissatisfaction cast a shadow on Alphonsus' conscience, but which did not darken his practical judgment. As proof, he dictated for Remondini on April 30:

During Passion Week I suffered from a deadly illness, but the Lord has allowed me to remain several days more upon this earth.

If the Jesuit Fathers make a big deal about my work, please tell them for me that the little that I know of Moral Theology (and it has been the field of my studies for more than thirty years) I have learned from them. Glory to Jesus and Mary!⁸

Two and a half years later, on October 12, 1758, he would write a notable letter to the Camaldolese Don Roberto:

It is lawful, and more than lawful, to follow the probable opinion, which is stable and well-founded [in favoring freedom], as compared to a more probable opinion favoring a precept....The basic reason for this is that the law remains doubtful.⁹

EQUIPROBABILISM

By small stubborn steps which we shall not retrace here, Alphonsus by 1762 in his *Breve dissertazione dell'uso moderato dell'opinione probabile* zeroed in on what his system would be—equiprobabilism. Let us remember that it does not deal with situations in which the method of prudence points out the way to follow, but rather those much rarer cases in which the undecided conscience does not know how to distinguish between obligation and freedom. Here are Alphonsus' three rules:

First case: The opinion favoring the law appears to be certainly more probable. We are then absolutely obliged to follow it and may not hold on to an opinion favoring freedom.

Such is required by the primacy of truth, the fear of God, and in faithfulness to the Gospel. Alphonsus thus rejects what he had written in 1758 to Don Roberto: he repudiates pure probabilism.

Second case: The opinion favoring freedom is probable, but no more; or is just as probable as that favoring the law. We are not allowed to follow it *simply because it is probable.*

The reason for this is that prudence requires more than probability. Probable? And what does probable mean here? a slim probability? an outside chance? or a probability favoring freedom? a fad? a matter of "professional practice," as it is said? No! Conscience must not get bogged down in subtleties; it must experience *personal* moral certitude. If the conscience cannot, it falls under the third and following case.

Third case: Two equally probable opinions come into conflict....The opinion favoring freedom, since it is as probable as that supporting the law, gives rise to a serious doubt about the existence of the law....We cannot then say that the law has been adequately promulgated. If the law has not been promulgated, it cannot oblige. An uncertain law cannot require a certain obligation.

We see here, in a refined form, the second reflex principle described in the *Dissertation* of 1749: "When the law is doubtful, freedom holds." Alphonsus thus emphasizes the value of humanity and its freedom. God is first and infinitely free. He wished to create humanity in relation to himself, in his image, therefore free. Since then, humanity is free in so far as a particular will of God has not been clearly revealed to the individual conscience. In other words, the general will of God is that humanity, his children, do what seems "good" to them, except in those cases in which God commands humanity to accomplish something or to avoid something. Still, it is necessary that God "proves" that a particular law exists for that law to be probable in the strictest sense of the term. For from the beginning, as God willed, freedom...is free, until the contrary is proven.

Thus the equiprobabilism of Alphonsus distinguishes three chief principles which, far from competing, balance and support one other: the principle of truth which, in the end, is God's; the principle of individual conscience on which each person will be judged; and the principle of freedom, which is humanity's. In summary, before the infinite dignity of the Divine Persons stands the eminent dignity of the human person.

Embodying the humanism of the Enlightenment and a Christian personalism—Alphonsus is very much of his times and ours.[10]

So how could the *Dictionnaire de la théologie catholique*, write in the article "Concina," col. 705, the following incredible abridgement of Alphonsus' "*doctrinal* career" (1746–1779)?:

The doctrinal career of Saint Alphonsus consists of two periods: in the first he was an ardent probabilist, as in the second he revealed himself to be a resolute probabiliorist.

This is as much as to say that the rainbow consists of two colors: an ardent violet and a resolute red.

An informed view, however, can easily follow the doctrinal development of the Doctor of Moral Theology going from a hesitant probabilism to a clear equiprobabilism, exactly half way to probabiliorism. He did not claim to have invented equiprobabilism, but to have discovered it. Once he arrived at equiprobabilism, Alphonsus was finally at rest, as was his friend the German Augustinian Euseb Amort (1692–1775).

Another incredible misinterpretation is the claim that the Alphonsian primacy of freedom is a "quest to escape" from the moral law. Here:

In casuistry everything occurs as though the subject, impelled by freedom, was always seeking *to escape universal laws* by means of particular circumstances, or at least to loosen the hold of such laws. The moralists themselves held as a principle to favor freedom over the law, for "freedom was the first property of human action," as Saint Alphonsus said. Within this context, in which the law is externally imposed upon acts, as in a deliberate clash of opposing forces, it is difficult to uphold the universality of the laws in the face of *a freedom that employs all its ingenuity in finding exceptions* through the use of extreme cases and that is constantly tempted to appeal to them *to break through the law itself.*

In the view of Saint Thomas, by contrast,…dealing with difficult and unusual cases is an exercise in judiciously applying laws, according to their spirit, rather than *seeking a loophole to escape from them.*[11]

So much for the patron saint of confessors and moral theologians! But let us leave the last word to an eminent Dominican, an expert at Vatican II and a specialist in moral theology:

Probabilism, besides being ill-distinguished from laxist excesses and compromised by them, was in its beginnings a serious concern for the Magisterium of the Church. And it remained such until the day when from the midst of moral theologies arose this monument called the *Moral Theology* of Saint Alphonsus. Within the swarming mass of opinions that were probable, more probable, less probable, certain, more certain, less certain, some clearly rigorist, others just as obviously lax, there emerged a collection of moral opinions that were truly certain, at equal distance from the extremes, and scrupulously weighed by the conscience of a saint. This was to render the Church a brilliant service. Many times praised and recommended by the Sovereign Pontiffs, and again recently by His Holiness Pius XII, Saint Alphonsus remains a Master *omni exceptione major*....No theologian can afford to ignore in resolving a concrete case what Saint Alphonsus thought. His authority is so great, so authentically established, that...it comprises one of the "common principles" to which it will always be permissible for a confessor to appeal when seeking a way out of doubt.[12]

DISPUTES

Once he had achieved his system, Bishop Liguori had by no means finished with his *Moral Theology*. One edition followed another at Remondini. They were always brought back to the drafting table and expanded with new instructions, dissertations and apologias. He wrote, "No matter how much a moralist tries to keep to the just mean in his writings, there will be those who contradict him!"[13]

The source of these contradictions was chiefly that he had built the whole of his immense work around the *Medulla* of Busenbaum. Busenbaum was one of those Jesuits that the hostility of competing religious orders, the jealousy of the secular clergy, the hatred of the Jansenists, and the family coalition of Bourbons now condemned to public disgrace. What the Jesuits could not be forgiven was their influence on the powerful, their educational hold on the young, their work in favor of the oppressed, and their gentle moral teachings. Hence Alphonsus faced a huge problem that he described to his printer-publisher on June 12, 1763:

Busenbaum has become odious to the whole world, or very nearly so. Now, to my distress, it is this blessed Busenbaum that I commented throughout my work. His name arouses the same horror as that of Luther! My confreres in the Congregation have thus advised me to suppress the text of this Jesuit and to make my *Moral Theology* a completely personal work....I am kicking myself for having taken Busenbaum as the basis of my commentaries, but who could have foreseen the storm that would assail the poor man?[14]

Busenbaum's name would disappear from the title as well as from the entire text.

Do all of the changes myself? The work would break me. I shall call upon two Fathers of my Congregation, and with them I hope to do it....With Busenbaum gone, the work will sell much better.

This was an argument no publisher could resist!

Alphonsus began the work during a forced rest at Nocera during August and September 1763. But he soon declared himself at his wits' end:

I have in fact had three Fathers at this task for several weeks. Sick as I am, I have also worked at it. In spite of that, we have not even finished the treatise on *Conscience*; and to do so, twenty days will not be enough. From this I conclude that to organize and put in shape all of the other treatises (many of which are much longer than that of *Conscience*) would take two years at the very least.[15]

At this time there was waiting in the wings of the publishing world, a learned Dominican moral theologian, Vincenzo Patuzzi (1700–1769). He was now ready to make his entrance. Resolved to strike a decisive blow against laxism, he amassed two hundred pages against Alphonsus' *Breve dissertatione* of 1762. Let us recall that Alphonsus, having at last achieved his moral system, put the finishing touches to equiprobabilism with the following fundamental affirmation: Since man was created free, an uncertain law cannot entail a certain obligation.

Hiding behind a pseudonym—the Very Reverend Professor Adelfo Dositeo—Patuzzi extolled the recent *Treatise on the Proximate Rule of Human Actions* by a "learned" author who was none other than himself! And as "the Italian Pascal," he seized upon the mere four pages of the Bishop of Sant'Agata that claimed to be weightier than the massive and invincible volumes of the rigorists. If only these four pages held up. But no! Patuzzi says Liguori understands neither the question nor the objections. Does Liguori even understand himself? And yet, how sure he is of himself! Illusionary certitude, dear Bishop! Culpable ignorance! Retract! Make amends for the scandal you have caused, still cause, and will continue to cause, unless you retract, lest you be cast into gehenna "where the worm does not die and the fire does not go out."

What is Patuzzi's argument? Before human beings existed there was the sovereign Legislator. Therefore, before our liberty, there is his law. Thus the law always holds; it has priority. Thence it follows that when doubt arises between law and freedom, one must *always follow the most certain opinion* (tutiorism) by choosing the law. Otherwise, one accepts the possibility of transgressing the law, and that (horror!) is sin.

Patuzzi's publisher was Remondini! Publishers are neither rigorists nor laxists; their business is to make books that will sell. At the same time he was printing Patuzzi's proofs, the printer was secretly sending the sheets to Alphonsus who could thus consider, accept, or refute his attacker's views.

Alphonsus wrote to Remondini on March 31, 1764:

I have promised to retract, and that publicly in writing, if anyone can show me the truth of an opinion contrary to mine. For the rest, on this matter I have consulted a number of learned and impartial men belonging to Father Patuzzi's order or that of [the Augustinian Father Lorenzo] Berti. Having dispassionately read my *Dissertation*, they have replied that what I have written is clear; that what is there is not an opinion, but a demonstration; and more than one scholar who was of an opposing view at first has retracted after having read my *Dissertation*, saying that it was irrefutable....

I highly esteem both Father Patuzzi and Father Berti for they are both erudite. But only God and the Church are infallible.

To say afterwards that I have written in passion or to follow the Jesuits is to charge me with an enormity, for that would be to claim that I know the truth but in order not to sacrifice the Jesuits or my own intention, I persist in defending a false opinion.

No. If I defend this opinion, it is because I am convinced that one in conscience must follow it. And I am also convinced that anyone who wants to oblige a penitent to follow a more certain opinion, when that penitent has confessed his sins and when, moreover, the opinions are equally probable, is not in a good state of conscience.

I do not think that I am even able without scruple to grant the faculty of hearing confessions to those who thus follow the rigid view. This is the truth that I confess before God. For the rest, let those who contradict me say what they will.[16]

The *Reply to the Short Dissertation of Bishop Liguori* (1764) was "mentally rather weak." Infallibly polite although allowing himself the occasional ironic smile, Bishop Liguori never granted an inch. The salvation of souls was too crucial to the debate. Hard on Patuzzi's heels, so to speak, Alphonsus came with two hundred and six pages of an *Apologia* against "the Very Reverend Professor who calls himself Adelfo Dositeo" (1764). Patuzzi replied to the answer. In response to this Alphonsus added an *Appendix* in 1765 to the *Apologia* which is chiefly interesting to us today for the following solemn affirmation:

Let my gainsayers accuse me all they want of yielding to stubbornness or passion; I allow them to say it. Truly, I do not know where I would find this passion. I can hope nothing more from this world. My advanced age and the illnesses that constantly assail me tell me that death is near. Moreover, it would clearly be mad if I refused to surrender my position in order to gain the praise of certain people or to make a name for myself. *What I have written I have written because before God who will soon judge me, I think thus.*

The duel petered out after a few more skirmishes. Still, in 1765 Alphonsus recast his last three publications into a "finished and structured" synthesis on the "right use of probable opinion." A dedication to his friend Clement XIII prefaced it. In this work he gave definitive form, enriched and sharpened by controversy, to his equiprobabilist position of 1762: as a son of God, made in the image of God, Man is free; confronted with a doubtful obligation, his freedom remains because it is certain; *the will of God is only imposed upon him if his individual conscience presents it to him as noticeably more probable.* It is on this last issue that since 1762 he had separated himself from the Jesuits, those probabilists to whom the rigorists wished to assimilate him in order to destroy, with them, both him and his missionary Congregation.

DIPLOMACY AND STEADFASTNESS

In fact, it was not long before a certain Diodato Targianni, adviser to the Viceroy of Palermo in Sicily, accused the Redemptorists of promoting Jesuitical morality and of handing out absolutions too freely. The witch hunt began in Portugal. On June 30, 1768, Alphonsus wrote to Remondini:

I have read in the *Avvisi* of Naples that in Portugal an ecclesiastic has been commissioned to prohibit moral theologies teaching a corrupt doctrine.

By corrupt moral theologies, they mean the whole of the Jesuits' moral theology. But, in truth, not all of the Jesuits' moral theology is corrupt. The works of Lugo, Suarez, Layman, Lessius, Castro Palao, etc., do not teach a corrupt doctrine....

Besides, my system of probabilism is not that of the Jesuits, because I do not allow the adoption of an opinion that is recognized as less probable, whereas Busenbaum, Lacroix, and almost all of the Jesuits allow it.

I wanted to tell you this so that you could inform others as need be, especially since in France they have burned a mass of works by the Jesuits, but they have not touched mine.

Who would ever have thought that one day the Jesuits
would be considered everywhere as assassins and rebels![17]

A year later it would be Alphonsus' turn. In the autumn of
1769 his *Moral Theology* was banned in Portugal. He suffered
greatly over this, but what was to be done? *Pazienza!* Patience!
His Congregation was not yet in Portugal!

The anti-Jesuit fever, however, was inspired by the Bourbon
faction and it rose ever higher. The Society was expelled from
one state after another dominated by the Bourbons in Europe,
America, and Asia. Portugal, which could not forgive them for
having supported the Guaranis in Paraguay, began in 1759.
France followed in 1764, then Spain in 1767. Charles III was
the Bourbon king of Spain; he also governed the two Sicilies
through his intermediary Tanucci. And it is difficult to imagine
how the Jesuit ghost haunted the days, nights, and prayers of
this contradictory man, Bernardo Tanucci. This oblate of the
Society of Jesus, whose confessor, like that of his wife and
daughter, was a Jesuit, wrote on April 29, 1767, to his friend
Luigi Viviani della Robbia:

> During Holy Week, happy is he who, like you, can leave
> the world for God, the unique good, the sole friend, the
> certain refuge, the only light of our minds. Scorn of for-
> tune, indifference towards honors [easily said by some-
> one who has them all], I owe them to my Master, my as-
> surance and my rest.

Fourteen lines later this mystical couplet yields to the following remonstrance:

> The Jesuits, paid assassins of Rome, traitors, plotters, cor-
> rupters of morality and Religion—they are the plagues of

Nations. They preach their infernal maxims against the finances of Sovereign Heads of State, against Kingship, Episcopacy, and the Gospel. They were finally unmasked in Spain after their assassination attempts in Portugal and after the inquests and trials in France.[18]

The following November 20, at nightfall, the troops surrounded the houses and institutions of the order founded by Saint Ignatius Loyola throughout the kingdom and dispatched the members of the Society of Jesus to the nearest ports.

From Agrigente in Sicily where the civil and religious powers were rigorists, the Redemptorist rector Father Pietro Paolo Blasucci was expelled, along with his priests, for laxist probabilism. A long correspondence followed between him and his superior. He wanted Alphonsus to change his system, to let it be clearly known that he was a probabiliorist, and to disassociate himself from every trace of Jesuit probabilism. For the rector major, Alphonsus, there were two realms here: that of pastoral and theological truth where he now took his stand and was not prepared to change, and that of his relations with an unendurable State in areas that did not concern it and about which it understood nothing. But in the latter case, he was a lawyer and a diplomat, and he was prepared to play a cunning game. Thus, in November 1768, he wrote to Blasucci:

> By the grace of God, I believe that I have clearly demonstrated the principle that a doubtful law does not obligate....It follows that when two opinions are equally probable the law does not obligate because it is doubtful.
>
> Before the publication of my book *On the Right Use of Probable Opinion* (1765), this point was not explained clearly enough; but today it is as clear as day—everybody

can see it. You can convince yourself of this by the letters I have had printed at the end of the volume.

After that, what does it matter that some fashionable scholars say the contrary? They do not see the heart of the matter and will say anything. Father Patuzzi has only confirmed my feeling about this, for out of the countless objections that he has raised, not one touched the heart of the debate, as even his friends have recognized.[19]

This covers the theological and pastoral truth. But you still do not want to be expelled from Sicily and want to label me as a probabiliorist? Go ahead. It was not the label that mattered, but the content. Besides, it would not be dishonest:

My own rule seems to me quite clear and certain. *When the opinion favoring the law is certainly more probable, I say that one cannot follow the less probable opinion.* Thus I am not a tutiorist, but a true probabiliorist....And in that I am opposed to the Jesuits' system.[20]

On August 5, 1772, Alphonsus again wrote to Blasucci:

Targianni is one of those who rage against probabilism without even knowing what the expressions "probable opinion," "more probable opinion," and "very probable opinion" mean.

Continue to repeat that I am, that we are all probabiliorists. And this is the truth, since I maintain that the probable opinion cannot be followed simply because it is probable. To act rightly, moral certitude is necessary. Probability alone is insufficient grounds for acting rightly. Even though I may not have written this in just these words, still I have explained it in an equivalent manner....

It is true that in Agrigente, as your letter shows, we cannot even use these words since they are partisans of tutiorism. This saddens me because poor souls are being lost. My God, in what unhappy times we live.[21]

In 1773, a certain Magli, a canon of Martina Franca in the region of Taranto, would fanatically wear out his pen trying to smear Alphonsus and his Institute. Villani feared the ruin of the Congregation over this. The Bishop, who judged this libel as being "full of baseless exaggerations," feared more for the ruin of souls. Consequently, he published a *Declaration of His System* in 1774.

Once again, I declare that I am not a probabilist, that I repudiate probabilism (no. 1)....What then of equiprobabilism? Recently, I have seen myself set by some people among the equiprobabilists, who are treated as immoral, licentious, people who would live lawlessly according to their own desires in order to abandon themselves to their carnal appetites and all the vices. Here we are treated as Manicheans, Epicureans, followers of Hobbes and Spinoza (no. 7)....No! Completely different from libertinism is the lawful liberty that is not bound by an unclear law (no. 44)....I shall not be persuaded to retract my system from which I recall the syllogism:
An insufficiently promulgated law does not obligate.
A doubtful law is not sufficiently promulgated.
Therefore, a doubtful law does not obligate (no. 55).

This is still, without the shameful word, the Alphonsian equiprobabilism of 1762.[22]

In 1767, after having retired from his bishopric and returned to Pagani, Bishop Liguori wrote again now at the age of eighty:

"I am no more a probabilist than I am a rigorist. I keep to the middle."[23]

This was no compromise, but a superior kind of balance. Besides, let us repeat, Alphonsus' moral system was only to be used if an examination of the concrete circumstances of an action still left one in a state of indecision. Also, the clash of systems was only the focal point of a more general conflict between rigorist, laxist, and "just mean" moralities.

THE MORAL SYSTEM AND THE DOCTRINE OF GRACE

A moral system and the doctrine of grace are linked because they both depend upon the idea one has of God and his liberality, of human beings and their liberty; and on the relationship between either divine love that is stingy, cold, and remote, or one that is generous, warm, and near.

Being familiar with the Gospels, an intimate of Jesus and Mary, and serving the masses, Alphonsus never let himself be trapped into any so-called natural theology created out of thin air by a philosopher. His doctrine of grace, like his moral system, does not descend from abstract reasoning. They arise rather from his long familiarity with God, his Word, and his People. Alphonsus explains himself in *A Short Treatise on Prayer,* a work of about twenty pages published in 1757, and at greater length in his very important spiritual and dogmatic work, *A Treatise on Prayer As the Great Means of Obtaining Eternal Salvation and the Graces We Desire from God* (1759). Quoting Saint John, he says:

God is love. Out of love he created man in his own image....
And God saw that it was good (Gen 1:26–31).
But sin came into the world!
Sin destroyed neither the love of God nor the nature of man.

Alphonsus spent his life in diagnosing sin and its ravages and healing them. Precisely because sin has not erased the image of God in any person and because God transcends all our miserable sins, his project of love has not changed: "God desires the salvation of everyone" (1 Tim 2:4). Also, "Christ died for everyone" (2 Cor 5:14–15, even for those who as free individuals stubbornly refused their Redemption.

Thus for all people all of the graces—God's help—necessary for salvation are available; but because God wishes them to be free, adults have to seek out and ask for these graces. Saint Augustine, whom the Jansenists misunderstood, writes: "God does not demand anything impossible. But when he commands, he exhorts you to do what you can and to ask for what you cannot." And the Council of Trent adds: "And he will help your effort." Alphonsus explains that what you are able to do you are able to do by the "efficacious grace" of the Lord "without whom you can do nothing" (Jn 15:5), but who in his good plan "gives both the desire and the action" (Philemon 2:13) to those who freely consent to it. If you think there is something you cannot do, at least you can ask for the ability to do it. The basic prayer, the cry addressed to God and Mary is easy. If God did not always give to everyone "sufficient grace" for this easy action, he would be demanding the impossible, paralyzing freedom, and destroying Christian hope. He would no longer be a father, but a tyrant. He would be denying his own Word when he said: "Pray always and never be discouraged" (Lk 18:1), and again: "Ask and ye shall receive" (Mt 7:7; Lk 11:9; Jn 16:24).[24]

CHAPTER 6

AGAINST THE STREAM

W hat sort of originality can one expect in a textbook? Did generations of moral theology textbooks, the *Institutiones Morales*, have any other aim than to plunge generations of seminarians into the mainstream of traditional teaching? It is true that this was a diversified teaching —rigorist in some, merciful in others, but essentially repetitive.

One might have thought that Alphonsus, overworked, teaching only occasionally, relying on Busenbaum, would go with the flow. But he had genius, and genius is creative. Moreover, he was a saint, and a saint is not a follower of men but of Jesus Christ.

As early as his *Adnotationes in Busembaum*, Alphonsus showed his individuality—his intention to use this famous textbook only as an excuse to be himself. The second edition, in two large volumes (1753–1755), is his personal *Theologia Moralis*. Nor did it freeze into this form; it continued to search for and create ways of being until its eighth edition (1779) when he was eighty-three years old. The final edition (1785) alone would be unaltered except that his picture was added (something he had always refused to do before), and Remondini's son, Giuseppe, a Freemason, introduced into the title-page device the Masonic triangle! Alphonsus, at ninety years of age

91

and nearly blind, would have to wait until he was in heaven to see it.

By looking at several important issues, let us point out Alphonsus' originality for his time.

LAW AND FREEDOM

Father Olivier de Dinechin, S. J., writes that "there are families of ethical thought. To follow a debate with many speakers or to understand a single speaker, it is very useful to have an overview of the field." He further postulates that there is "a range of basic ethical positions centered on three large families that are themselves internally diversified." These are the ethics of religious traditions, those derived from the Enlightenment, and agnostic ethics. Since Alphonsus cannot be associated with agnostic ethics, there remain the Western monotheistic (Judaism, Christianity, and Islam) religious ethics and the ethics of the Enlightenment.

Looking at religious ethics, one observes that they all believe that

morality is founded and centers on a *God-given law* that is known [by Revelation. Revelation] is fixed in Sacred Scriptures and in the *traditions which interpret it*.... Whence is derived a *basic ethical attitude that is respectful and conservative*. As for freedom, religious traditions do not separate it from the *call of God to choose the good*.[1]

The philosophers of the Enlightenment had little patience with theological morality. Of them, Paul Hazard has written: "Morality based on religious dogma had been rejected as being too rigid, and as deriving from an authority external to man."[2]

The eighteenth and nineteenth centuries saw the rise of *Enlightenment ethics* which, as Father de Dinechin says,

have unquestionably shaped our culture, including Christianity....The ethical assertions common to these ways of thinking can be outlined as follows:

1. *Man is the subject of morality.* He is endowed with reason and free will and is fundamentally *autonomous.*
2. *Reason can and must enlighten* the behavior of man by showing him what is true or false, good or bad. This applies as much to the customs and social laws which he inherits and can transform as it does to his individual behavior.
3. *Experience* supplies reason with greater means of judging than does authority, which is always inclined to arbitrariness, or tradition, which is condemned to repetition.
4. Freedom is essentially *the free will of the individual conscience,* which is able to judge rightly to the extent that it detaches itself from every "prejudice," whether personal, social, historical, cultural, or other.
5. *Reference to a Divinity* may enter the realm of reason but only to the extent that it is agreeable to reason.[3]

Dinechin charts the following main currents in Enlightenment ethics: the ethics of *duty*, whether subject to God or to principles; *humanistic* ethics based on man himself and therefore rejecting "pure idea" separate from concrete reality; *utilitarianism* and *anarchism*.

Into which category are we to place Saint Alphonsus' *Theologia Moralis*—into religious ethics or Enlightenment ethics? Clearly, because of the use of the word *theology*, it would belong in the first category. Alphonsus discusses the Ten Commandments and the requirements for the sacraments. But it is also one of the best examples of how "Enlightenment ethics have unquestionably influenced Christianity." Of the five criteria Dinechin lists for classifying Enlightenment ethics, Alphonsus would deny only the last. He accepts and integrates into his Christian thought the claims made about man, reason, experience, and freedom of conscience, all of which are Christianity's true and legitimate offspring. To this extent, Alphonsus Liguori's morality belongs to the second category—that of the Enlightenment—while keeping the best in the first category.

If one had to choose further between the different "families" that Dinechin distinguishes in Enlightenment thought, Alphonsus would be at home in the *ethics of duty*—but this duty is the quest for and the accomplishment of the will of God—and in *humanistic ethics* inasmuch as it does not seek first for "principles" and "pure ideas" but for "concrete realities."

What then of the "eternal" or "universal laws" of some metaphysicians? It could only be God Himself. And it only has moral importance insofar as it concerns persons. Now, the only divine law is freedom in love, for "God is love" and love is freedom, or it does not exist.

The first law of humanity created in the image of God is thus also freedom in love—in the love of other persons, beginning, of course, with the Divine Persons, to the extent that they know them. From this is derived the priority of the individual conscience. Concina, Patuzzi, and the probabiliorists fought for a *sui generis*, "objective" moral truth external to human beings, while Alphonsus only recognized a subjective, "personalized," existential moral truth internal to the conscience. As Father Häring says:

The role of conscience is central to morality in the patron saint of moral theologians. Against the dominant tendencies of his time, he firmly stressed respect for the conscience, even when it was, in good faith, in error.[4]

Two examples can be given of quite different typical cases:

Can a confessor absolve a penitent who is following a probable opinion that is contrary to a more probable opinion held by the confessor? Not only can he, but he is bound to do so under pain of grave sin....For he is not to judge the *opinions* of the penitent, unless they are clearly false, but his *dispositions*, that is to say, his contrition and his good intent....Once confessed, the well-disposed penitent has a strict right to absolution.[5]

Moreover, in choosing an opinion, when it is a question of removing a penitent from the danger of formal sin, the confessor must often follow the most tolerant opinions, to the degree that Christian prudence allows him to do so.

In other words, do not oblige the penitent to follow the best way if you are not sure that he would take it.

If, however, the penitent's opinion places him in close proximity to the danger of formal sin, then the confessor absolutely must advise him to follow the stricter opinion. I say *advise* because if the penitent holds a truly probable opinion and wishes to follow it, he cannot be refused absolution, since, by his confession which he has already made, he has acquired the right to receive absolution.[6]

The second example of the primacy of the truth of the ("subjective") conscience over "objective" truth is:

A confessor [realizes that his penitent is committing sins the gravity of which he is unaware]; if he foresees that his admonition would do no good, must he nevertheless warn him? No. The confessor can and must leave him in good faith. Of two evils it is necessary to choose the lesser. When the choice lies between material and formal sin, one must at all costs avoid the latter, for it alone God punishes because by it alone is He offended. But what then of the truth? Certainly, the confessor cannot deceive his penitent *if the latter asks him*. But he is not only a teacher, he is a physician. And his faculty to hear confessions is first of all a ministry of charity. Is the truth to be sacrificed then? In no way. He does not choose between truth and charity. He practices charity toward the penitent and towards God [who will not be formally offended] without doing injury to the truth. He does not speak it [because it is not good to utter every truth]....A single formal sin is more serious than all the material sins together.[7]

The saint describes an extreme case:

Usually, peasants know that rape is a more serious sin than simple fornication. In contrast, they are unaware of the difference between the evil of fornication and the greater evil of adultery. Thus, with those who are habituated to this vice, it is inexpedient to warn them of its greater seriousness when one can foresee that such an admonition would serve no useful purpose, except to make them commit a double sin (fornication and adultery) when they yield to their inclinations.[8]

"Ah ha!" someone might think, "that simply adds fuel to the fire of those who accused Alphonsian casuistry of doing away with the law itself!"

But surely not! Is not the first "law" that of charity—toward God whom we spare offense and toward individuals whom we prevent from falling deeper into sin?

And how could the morality of *Saint* Alphonsus not be a morality of *holiness*? *"Agere sequitur esse,"* actions follow being as the scholastic maxim says.

A MORALITY OF HOLINESS

When Alphonsus was laying the foundations of his doctrinal edifice around 1743, he had no intuition of his future vocation as moral theologian of the Universal Church. He thus began with a confessors' textbook as one might start out to write a medical dictionary and end up creating a world health organization. He just could not be satisfied with just a textbook on pathology.

As a man of God and a spiritual son of Saint Francis de Sales, he could never be content with only marking the boundaries between sin—both venial and mortal—and the Christian life. From childhood he had experienced the inner call to permanent conversion, to holiness; and when he was a young lawyer, to the mystical life of union with God. As a young priest in the slums of Naples, he dared to preach this call to the miserable sinners found there; and as a confessor and spiritual director, he saw them rise toward perfection. He had the same gratifying experience with the forsaken country people.

That is partly the reason why he was soon dissatisfied with his *Adnotationes in Busembaum.* He rearranged his *Theologia Moralis* into two volumes—the dates, 1753–1755, are noteworthy—and included in it his pastoral treatise, *Praxis Con-*

fessarii, without which, he wrote, the *Moral Theology* would be "truncated and incomplete." He explains his reasons in section 121:

> The confessor cannot be content with *rooting out* vice. He had also a *mission to the nations to build and to plant* (Jer 1:10) virtues...to encourage spiritual beings to devote themselves completely to God. A perfect soul is more pleasing to God than a thousand mediocrities. Furthermore, when the confessor observes a penitent living without grave sin, he must use all his means to impel him towards the perfection of Divine Love.

Alphonsus explains how the "prudent confessor" introduces penitents to and helps them progress in prayer, in the transformation of the heart, submission to the will of God, and in forming generous intentions.

A third of this "Confessor's Textbook" is dedicated to the step-by-step ascent to holiness. In Alphonsus' thought, morality is closely bound up with mystical and dogmatic theology. He himself is both a great mystic and a great dogmatician. His moral theology, which grants the last word to conscience and reason, is thus the opposite of "rationalism."

That is why he wrote and published in tandem with his great *Theologia Moralis*, and in the same years, delightful little pamphlets for less-educated people with smaller wallets. They were short treatises, inspired by the Gospels, on the moral theology of baptismal perfection. In 1754 *The Way to Converse Always and Familiarly with God* came out:

> Does God love you? Love him....Your God is ever near you, nay, within you....In the morning He is there to hear a word of love or trust, to receive...the offering of your

whole day—acts of virtue and good works you promise to engage in to please Him, pains you declare yourself ready to suffer for His glory and love….At that very moment, He utters to you His gentle commandment: "You shall love the Lord your God with all your heart."…During the day renew often the offering of yourself to God: "Lord, I am here; do with me what seems good to you. Grant that I may know your will, for I desire to fulfil it completely."[9]

The same year (1754) saw *Regole per ben vivere*, later reworked in *Rules for a Christian Life* (1759). The purpose was to advance the believer through the struggle with temptation, the sacraments, and the life of prayer to the virtues of humility, mortification, brotherly love, patience, conformity to the will of God, for "all holiness consists in loving God; and to love God is to do His will.[10]

Conformity to the Will of God (1755) is explained in an invaluable thirty-page pamphlet. "All for God" is the height of Christian morality:

Because he who gives his will to God gives all. Whether by alms we give our goods in charity, or our blood in self-flagellation, or by fasting our sustenance, we give God only a part of what we have. But to give him our will is to give all. Only then have we the right to say to God "Lord, I am poor, but I give you all that I can: My will is yours; I have nothing more to give you."[11]

Each of those three short works went through more than five hundred editions. They prepared the way for what was to be the Bishop of Sant'Agata's moral theology masterpiece on a popular way to holiness, *The Practice of the Love of Jesus Christ* (1768). There Alphonsus asserts the principle that holiness is not a special privilege. Every Christian can and must strive for it:

> It is a very wrong to say that God does not wish us all to be perfect. Saint Paul says "For this is the will of God, your sanctification" (1 Thes 4:3), but each according to his state: the religious as religious, the priest as priest, married people in the state of matrimony, the merchant as merchant, the soldier as soldier....Surely, if we rely upon God, and through constant effort, we will gradually arrive at where so many saints through divine grace have gone.[12]

In line with this teaching, Alphonsus desired that his missionaries, having preached conversion to sinners, also initiate them into the life of perfection. They ought never to leave the people they have evangelized without having formed them in the practices of true piety to strengthen resolve and cultivate divine love, thus assuring perseverance. But even more than perseverance, holiness is needed. For this reason the essential practice to be implanted after every mission is daily meditation, the absolute prerequisite to Christian perfection.

Alphonsus asked the most of people and had no qualms in teaching everyone, as does the Gospel, that the children of God must "be perfect, therefore, as your heavenly Father is perfect" (Mt 5:48). He explains what this perfection is and why the definition of holiness applies to all Christians, because its author is the Divine Master. As Jesus replied to the teacher of the law who asked him what was the first commandment, it is "to love God with all your heart."

It follows that the highest art—that which is necessary to teach to everyone—is the art of loving God. This art consists precisely in *detaching* one's heart from every creature and from one's own personality and attaching it to God, to Jesus, and uniting it so closely to the will of Jesus that the transformed person can cry out with Saint Paul: "It is no longer I who live, but it is Christ who lives in me" (Gal 2:20).

Detachment and attachment, or *union*, are the two key words in all of Alphonsian spirituality—the height of its moral theology.

THE ADVOCATE OF SINNERS

A Dominican from the Ardennes, Charles-René Billuart (1685–1757), was one of the greatest commentators on the *Summa* of Saint Thomas. In the middle of the eighteenth century, Billuart published a nineteen-volume *Summa S. Thomae* in Liège between 1746 and 1751 (again, notable dates), and makes the following statement which clearly sets Alphonsus against the mainstream:

> From 1699 until the present year of 1747, very few have written in favor of probabilism. In contrast, many have written in favor of probabiliorism. If we speak of theologians, as much those who write as the others, every day we see a vast number leave probabilism for probabiliorism, while no one is going from probabiliorism to probabilism. This is so much the case that if in 1710 Father Henno was able to say that in his time there were twenty probabiliorists for every probabilist, today we can say that there are forty probabiliorists for every probabilist.[13]

At the very time when one of the most informed theologians in the world was observing the rapid rise in rigorism, our future Doctor of the Church was putting the finishing touches on his two probabilistic *Dissertations*, thus reacting to Genet and official teachings (1749 and 1755). He went to an extreme and retracted, but only halfway, as we have seen. Alphonsus never identified the sinner with sin. No more than did Christ. Sin is an absolute evil, but the sinner is basically good. In the Gospels, Jesus shows no tolerance for sin ("Go your way, and from now on do not sin again") but is completely merciful to the sinner ("Neither do I condemn you"). "All the tax collectors and sinners were coming near to listen to him. And the pharisees and scribes were grumbling and saying, 'This fellow welcomes sinners.'"[14]

Such was Alphonsus' obsession, an obsession to which Tannoia bears witness on innumerable occasions. Do the preachers and the confessors continue the work of the Savior, or do they have another "profession"?[15] "He [Alphonsus] wanted sinners to be received with open arms. Jesus, he said, did not do otherwise."[16]

We do not see Christ driving away the black sheep, but rather bringing the lost sheep back on his shoulders. Following Christ's example, Alphonsus especially fought delays in absolution, which were the norm and which entailed refusing the sacraments to sinners. He relied again on experience:

Some confessors, holding to severity, only lead souls along the path of rigor. Absolutely excessively, they hold that all backsliders will go from bad to worse if they are absolved before they have mended their ways. As for myself, I should like to ask these "teachers" who are telling me what to do: Do all the backsliders who are sent away without absolution and deprived of sacramental grace become stronger and capable of amending themselves? How many of these poor unfortunates have I myself encountered who, because they have been refused absolution, have fallen into despair and have strayed for years, despising the sacraments?[17]

This is not to say that Alphonsus was opposed to any delay in absolution, but he militated against the then current practice of treating such delays as a panacea.

[On the contrary,] if it is a question of restoring the goods of another, do not let the penitent be absolved until he has actually made restitution, if he is able, because once he has been absolved, he will find it very difficult to do so.[18]

This is a special and decisive case in which Alphonsus would never tone down his assertion. Real mercy here is not to be merciful. But elsewhere mercy always has the last word, as in the Gospels. At the time this was quite revolutionary: "For Concina one of the sources of corruption in moral theology is too great a trust in divine mercy."[19]

The source of Alphonsus' pastoral theology is a threefold trust: in the mercy of God, in the good will of the sinner who has gone to the trouble of going to confession, and in the transforming and sanctifying grace of the sacraments of reconciliation and the Eucharist. This demonstrates the quality of the faith and the confidence in humanity. It is the opposite of Jansenism. He repeats:

Do not frighten penitents by delaying their absolution from month to month, as is the fashion. This does not help them, but results in their loss. When a sinner acknowledges his sins and despises them, he must not be left alone to fight against temptation. He must be helped, and the best help is the grace of the sacraments. The sacrament compensates for the failing powers of the sinner. It is the teaching of the Jansenists to defer absolution from month to month. Far from drawing people to the sacraments, they make the sacraments useless to them....Do many sinners lack a

sufficient disposition for absolution? Then let them be
inspired with feelings of repentance by vividly presenting
to them the gravity of sin, its offense against God, Para-
dise lost, and Hell opening beneath their feet. In this one
sees the charity of the confessor. There are some who
would make of sinners so many faggots for the fires of
Hell! Let them rather give the sinner a helping hand![20]

Such was the missionary's motto. He nevertheless recognized and recounted in detail the cases in which reconciliation
could not be granted for lack of the necessary dispositions. Yet
he also stated that the confessor should strive to create such
dispositions and should settle for even a small hope that they
were present. This was the pastoral theology of the saint who
rejoiced in his old age that—let it be stressed again—he never
refused absolution.[21] Besides, he was well aware that some de-
mons "can only be cast out by prayer and fasting"—to which
he added hair shirts and self-flagellations. But he did not read
about this in Genet.

Besides those who were in possession of someone else's property, the kinds of sinners that could not be absolved before ef-
fective amendment were habitual sinners and backsliders. "By
habitual sinner," Alphonsus explains, "we mean one who confesses for the first time a vicious habit." Should we wait for
him to correct himself before absolving him? No.

He can very well be absolved before any amendment, provided he seriously intends to amend himself. [Why?] He
has come to the sacrament: do not impute to him the intention of making a sacrilege of it. Besides, his spontane-
ous confession is a sign of contrition.[22]

The backslider is he who, after confession, has fallen
again into the same sins. Should he be given absolution

unconditionally each time? No. Should absolution be delayed until a long period has passed without backsliding? Again, no. This is intolerable strictness; it also ignores grace, which has no need of time. It is sufficient that the confessor have a prudent assurance of the good intentions of his penitent.[23]

But would not delaying absolution be a better remedy?...Concina, Juenin and Merbesius say that this remedy is necessary....As for myself, I think that if the backslider again falls into sin, not by voluntarily placing himself at risk but by internal weakness, it is rarely needful to defer absolution if he is well disposed....Sacramental grace will do him more good than a delay in absolution.[24]

In the end, on this matter of conferring or delaying absolution, let each confessor direct himself according to the light God gives him. What is certain is that those who are too lenient and those who are too strict are both in error....As for which of them ought to act more scrupulously—I have no idea.[25]

Even after a painful delay, a strict confessor finally conferred an absolution usually flavored with a bitter penance. The Council of Trent did not judge this wrong. In *Homo Apostolicus*, Alphonsus begins by faithfully citing the Council.

The priests of the Lord, guided by their lights and their prudence, must impose beneficial and appropriate satisfactions corresponding to the nature of the sins and the strength of the penitents, lest by shutting their eyes to the sins and showing too much indulgence to the penitents, they inflict punishments that are too light for weighty crimes and thus become partakers of the sins of others (see 1 Tim 5:22). Let them not lose sight of the fact that the satisfaction they impose is not only a defense for a new life and a remedy against weakness, but also a chastisement and a punishment for previous sins. For the power of the keys was conferred upon priests not only to loosen but also to bind (see Mt 16:19; 18:18; Jn 20:23). Such was the belief and the teaching of the ancient Fathers.[26]

In fact, in quoting this text Alphonsus stops halfway through the passage. He does not have the heart to brandish Tridentine "chastisement" and "punishment" against sinners. Rather, he immediately deduces:

Thus the extent of the penance is remitted by the Council to the confessor's judgment, to his "lights" and "prudence." As a result, penance can be reduced for numerous reasons.[27]

He details these reasons over seven pages, calling to the rescue Saint Thomas, Gerson, Cajetan, Saint Antoninus, and so on, and even Saint Charles Borromeo.

He also interprets the words of the Council. "Appropriate" penances are those which are "appropriate" to the sinners' weakness.

[If this were not the case,] what would happen? They would do nothing and therefore judge themselves guilty of a new sin. They would think that their confession was null and fall back into their previous miserable life. Frightened by the burden of penances, they would hold confession in horror and continue to wallow in their sins.[28]

Besides being "appropriate," satisfactions must also be, according to the Council of Trent, "beneficial" and "salutary." What does this mean according to Alphonsus?

Frequent attendance upon the sacraments, mental prayer, alms? Experience shows that these are ill suited for those who are little or not at all used to them. But, in general, the following are good for everyone: to make an act of contrition each evening and to repeat each morning the saying of Saint Philip Neri: "Lord, keep me from betraying you today"; to visit the Blessed Sacrament and an image of the Holy Virgin every day, asking them for perseverance; to recite the rosary; to say three Hail Marys morning and evening with the petition: "Help me not to offend God today" (this is the penance that I give most often to those who are not in the habit of doing it); at night, when in bed, to say "Had I been cast into the fires of Hell" or "The day will come when I shall die in this bed." Saint Francis de Sales warns not to load the penitent with too many things lest he be overburdened or frightened.[29]

All of Saint Alphonsus is there—the theologian of grace and perseverance through petition and prayer. As for the "punishments" and "chastisements" enjoined by the Council of Trent, he does not breathe a word. "Let us try," he said, "to inspire horror not of penance but of sin."[30]

THE BREAD OF THE STRONG FOR THE WEAK

Confronted with the mercy of Him "who came not for the righteous, but for sinners," pharisees have risen up from time to time within the Church. In the seventeenth century they were the Jansenists and most especially Genet's friend, Antoine Arnauld, the author of the famous treatise *On Frequent Communion* (1643). Recognizing it as a tempting sweet laced with cyanide, Saint Vincent de Paul explodes in a letter of September 10, 1648:

This book is powerfully diverting everyone from an obsession with Holy Communion….In fact, does it not highly praise the piety of those who wish to defer Communion to the end of their lives because they feel they are unworthy to approach the Body of Jesus Christ….Had I followed M. Arnauld's book, not only would I have renounced Mass and Holy Communion forever, I would have held the sacrament in horror. He presents it, with respect to those who commune with the ordinary dispositions approved by the Church, as a snare of the devil and as a soul-sickening poison, and he treats those who approach it in this state as little better than dogs, swine, and Antichrists.[31]

Arnauld's anti-eucharistic treatise was never directly condemned. Still, it caused a massive desertion from the Holy Table for a century and a half in Europe, and this in spite of Tradition and the Council of Trent. The servant who would search out the highways and byways for guests to attend the royal banquet was Alphonsus Liguori.[32] He would write:

There is nothing that so ruins souls and the Church as error disguised by the specious rigor of evangelical perfection. These evildoers are chiefly the Jansenists. They are more dangerous than Calvin and Luther because one can be taken in by their false pretenses.

And he repeated:

Above all, one must beware of Antoine Arnauld. He will sell you holiness. While he appears to seek only purity and perfection for admission to Communion, he has no other aim than to separate the faithful from the sacrament, the only cure for our weakness.[33]

One day he said:

We have reached the point where modern spiritual directors strive only to turn the faithful away from the sacraments, as if the only way to God were to separate souls from God. I wish that certain confessors had, to worthily celebrate the Mass, half the good dispositions they require of their penitents.[34]

Let us not think that Alphonsus was overdramatizing. His disciple and friend, Father Alessandro Di Meo (1726–1786), an historian whose *Annals of the Kingdom of Naples* was admired throughout Europe, reveals how reality surpassed fiction:

One would not believe the levels of fanaticism reached by many priests whose duty, from their state and function, had been to defend the cause of God and souls. Innumerable Communions have been publicly refused for the sole reason of not having abstained long enough from the sacrament. Many are those who have been insulted before the altar because they wished to communicate during the week. Some parish priests made up lists of those they wish to approach the Holy Table and have them read it aloud at Mass, calling by name those whom they deign worthy to receive this favor. Or else, those who wish to communicate have been asked for a written testimonial from their spiritual directors stating that they were worthy.[35]

Alphonsus taught that

Jesus Christ alone received the Eucharist worthily because God alone is able worthily to receive God....The consensus of the Doctors is that it is better to commune every day out of love than to abstain out of respect.

He distinguishes between weekly Communion, daily Communion, and frequent Communion. By the last he means several times a week. For him, Sunday Communion is not frequent. Following his "fathers," Philip Neri and Gaétan de Thiene, he urges daily Communion, thus setting himself off from the Jesuits Suarez, Lugo, Toledo, and Vasquez, and from his teacher Francis de Sales, all of whom considered frequent Communion to be monthly or bimonthly. Alphonsus writes:

> A spiritual director cannot without scruple refuse frequent or even daily Communion to a soul who desires it to grow in the love of God....And should such a soul fall into some voluntary venial sin through sheer weakness and repents... why should he be refused Communion?...The weaker a person feels, the more that person ought to be fed with the Bread of the strong.[36]

He recalls the Council of Trent's wish that everyone who assists at the Sacrifice of the Mass should participate in Communion:

> The Roman Catechism thus instructs the parish priest in his duty to exhort urgently the faithful to communicate not only frequently, but daily. Indeed, it imposes an obligation to teach them that the soul, like the body, needs to be nourished every day.[37]

Five years after the appearance of *Istruzione e Pratica* (1757)—*Homo Apostolicus* (1759) in Latin—a certain Don Gennaro Andolfi of the Neapolitan clergy published under the pseudonym Cipriano Aristasio a *Lettera* in which he attacked Alphonsus' teaching on Communion. Meanwhile, in May–June 1762, Clement XIII summoned the recently nominated bishop of Sant'Agata dei Goti to Rome for a number of lengthy interviews. The pope invited him to refute the *Lettera* of Aristasio. While still in Rome, Bishop Liguori immediately wrote and had printed a thirty-five page *Riposta*. Don Andolfi responded with a *Replica alla Riposta* in which he based his rigorism on the Fathers and the Doctors of the Church. As if, on a selective reading from an a priori position, one could not make them say anything or the opposite of anything! Overburdened with work in his new diocese, the bishop had Father Di Meo respond. The latter produced a learned volume—*Confutazione della Lettera e Replica*—four-hundred pages long and bristling with notes. "Don't pass me off as a scholar!" Alphonsus told him; and always thinking of the poor and the poorly educated, it became a twenty-three page pamphlet, *Riposta apologetica* (1764), which sent Aristasio back to his desk for a final *Difesa* (1765).

Out of this polemic, we need to keep in mind two of Alphonsus' assertions:

Aristasio regards weekly Communion as frequent. For me, weekly Communion is neither frequent nor rare. It is what is appropriate for anyone who desires to live in God's grace.

Ordinarily speaking, a spiritual director ought to grant weekly Communion to persons he finds disposed for sacramental absolution.[38]

In other words, whoever is in a state of grace is "invited to the Supper of the Lord."

But is the marital state, ordinarily speaking, compatible with the state of grace?

FREEDOM TO MARRIED PEOPLE

After painstaking analysis, Professor Delumeau concluded in *Sin and Fear* that

The ecclesiastical discourse on sex of the thirteenth through the sixteenth centuries was quantitatively important....Never had an entire civilization been subjected to such an investigation of sexuality, especially within marriage.[39]

Because of his delicacy and reserve, Alphonsus did not participate in this lusty enthusiasm. One might be surprised to learn that Alphonsus' missions included no sermons on lust or the duties of the marriage bed. Out of the three-thousand pages of Gaudé's edition of the *Theologia Moralis*, only ninety-three are concerned with the sixth and ninth commandments and with sexuality in marriage. There is no hint here of obsession. But beyond this, Alphonsus' knowledge and experience of human beings allowed him to offer freedom to married people.

First, let us rid ourselves of one of the theoretical problems in which speculative thinkers have taken such delight. This is the matter of sexual pleasure within marriage. Protestantism marked the lowest point of European pessimism in the sixteenth and seventeenth centuries. Luther, the married Reformer, wrote: "I say that flesh and blood, having been corrupted by Adam, are conceived and are born in sin...and that conjugal duty is never accomplished without sin."[40]

This is Saint Augustine at his most characteristic and worst. Caesarius of Arles, Gregory the Great, and Thomas Aquinas also joined into this tidal wave of opinion that could not be stopped by the few attempts to stem the tide.[41]

How many centuries, how much ink, and how many brains went into the statement by the Jesuit Tomás Sánchez (1550–

1610) that "the conjugal act undertaken for pleasure *alone* is a venial sin"? On March 2, 1679, Blessed Innocent XI "canonized" this proposition by condemning its opposite, i.e.: "The conjugal act undertaken for pleasure *alone* (*ob solam voluptatem*) is without any sin, even a venial one" (DS 2109).

Whether he wanted to or not, Saint Alphonsus could only submit to the authority of what would be called in the nineteenth century the Magisterium. Thus we find him repeating:

> It is certain that it is illicit to use marriage for pleasure *alone*, as concluded from Innocent XI's condemnation of proposition 9. Nevertheless, in the common view, it is only a venial sin.[42]

The little word *alone* disarms this little smoke bomb. Aside, perhaps, from some brutish spouse, who would exercise conjugal rights *for pleasure alone*? Who would exclude every other end, such as love or the simple remedy of desire (*remedium concupiscentiae*), which has always been recognized as one of the legitimate ends of marriage? Who would make pleasure the *ultimate and exclusive* purpose of the act?

Let us leave these questions and get down to facts. One of Alphonsus' pastoral comments was contradicted in the nineteenth century by a number of decrees from the Sacred Penitentiary, but is worth considering: "Ordinarily speaking, it is not appropriate for the confessor to ask spouses about the sins of the marriage bed. Let him not speak of them, unless he is asked."[43]

Alphonsus then begins writing on married life with the following words:

> Is the conjugal act licit? It is, of itself, licit and virtuous. And this proposition is one of faith, as is clear from

1 Corinthians 7: Let the husband fulfil his duty toward his wife [and vice versa].[44]

And so let us have done with the Augustinian distinction made between the two partners, one of whom yields upon request and does not sin and the one who requests and does sin. "For the same purposes that make marriage lawful also legitimate the request for union."[45] But what ends, or purposes, make marriage lawful? Saint Augustine's answer would hold sway for centuries. He explains that the three merits of marriage are fecundity (*proles*), fidelity (*fides*), and indissolubility (*sacramentum*, the "vow"). But these three meritorious effects are not sufficient reason to allow carnal union. Only the actual intention to procreate legitimates the conjugal act.

As we have just said, Alphonsus does not agree with this restriction. In several classic pages he describes the ends of marriage otherwise.

Marriage can be considered to have *three categories of ends*: essential intrinsic ends, accidental intrinsic ends, and accidental extrinsic ends.

There are two *essential intrinsic ends*: mutual giving, with the duty of giving oneself to bodily union, and the indissolubility of the bond. Likewise, there are two *accidental intrinsic ends*: procreation of children and satisfaction of the sexual instinct. There can, however, be many *accidental extrinsic ends:* peace between families, a great opportunity that is not to be missed, etc. This means:

It is certain that, first, whoever aspires to marriage while excluding its essential intrinsic ends—the gift of the body and indissolubility—will not only sin, but the marriage will be null. This is the common teaching, with Saint Thomas at its head.

It is certain that, secondly, whoever excludes the *accidental intrinsic ends* will contract not only a valid, but sometimes a licit marriage. (Take, for example, an elderly man who no longer can hope for children nor has concupiscence to assuage.)

But what of someone who marries with the satisfaction of his carnal appetites as his principal goal?

This person will contract a valid marriage...because marriage was instituted by God not only to bring children into the world, but as a remedy for concupiscence, as is proved by the words of the Apostle (1 Cor 7:2). *"But because of cases of sexual immorality, each man should have his own wife and each woman her own husband."* This is not simple tolerance, but a counsel....

If there is peril of incontinence, Saint Paul not only allows marriage, but he absolutely urges it, saying in verse 9 that *"For it is better to marry than to be a flame with passion."* And again, addressing spouses (v. 5): "Do not deprive one another...so that Satan may not tempt you because of your lack of self-control." If married couples can request the conjugal act for the sole end of avoiding incontinence, then they can also marry with this same goal.[46]

Let us stress that Alphonsus as a "casuist" first consults Scripture when it offers an answer to a moral case.

On the *ends of marriage*, he does not hesitate to contradict Saint Augustine, Saint Thomas, and (almost) the whole Roman law tradition reaffirmed in the *Codex Juris Canonici* of 1917 (cc. 1013 and 1082) and by Pius XI in *Casti connubii*. "Mar-

---

riage is valid," Alphonsus maintains, "even when there is the intention to avoid having children."[47] He proves this by an objective interpretation of Saint Paul and by the juridical practice of the Church. Ivory-tower theologians seem to be unaware that the Church has always recognized the marriages of elderly or sterile (though not impotent) persons as valid. Now, there is more theology in the practice of the Church than in all the folio volumes of the doctors.

What is certain is that fecundity belongs to the *intrinsic* structure of marriage and the conjugal union, but not to its *essence*. There may be good grounds for demoting it to the second rank—first of all, the satisfaction of sexual desire—or "even, occasionally, to exclude it as an intention, for example in the case of a poor man who fears the burden of too many children."[48]

Marriage is considered chiefly and in itself as an expression of the mutual gift of persons in an "irrevocable pact of love which includes the right of physical union."[49]

Such are the ends of marriage. Its *use* is governed by its ends.

Jansenists and rigorists allowed as licit only such sexual relations as were justified by the intention to procreate or by the just demand of the partner. In a few words, Saint Alphonsus gives a liberating answer. Every goal that justifies marriage also justifies the uses of marriage: procreation (Alphonsus does not demand the intention to procreate; he even admits that some people, while using marriage, can desire not to have children); a remedy for concupiscence; psychological and physical health, and even pleasure, provided that it is not made the ultimate end of one's existence. Here again rigorism and pessimism are defeated. Not only are married partners to live any longer obsessed by sin, but in his *Practica di amar Gesù Cristo* [*Practice of the Love of Jesus Christ*] Alphonsus calls upon them to realize perfection and even to attain holiness in their conjugal life: "God wishes that all become holy, but each in his own state...married people in the state of matrimony." [50]

In order to marry, however, couples must meet. Even though Alphonsus is so humane toward married people, he is *uncompromising when it comes to those who are engaged.* Why? I have found nine writings by Alphonsus and two pages by Tannoia on this matter. [51] The writings shed light on each other. Rather, the oldest text in *Reflections useful for Bishops* (1745, first English edition 1890) throws a harsh light (and one appropriate to contemporary life) on the others.

When engaged couples visit each other, occasions arise favorable to innumerable sins. It is therefore fitting that in every diocese the parish priests be ordered not to accept an engagement party unless assured that the couple will marry within a short period of time. For if the engagement is made long before the marriage, as is done in many places, the fiancés feel free to move into the houses of their future spouses and then live constantly in disgrace with God. This is why it would be good to reserve [for the bishop's absolution] not only the sins of carnal union and cohabitation (i.e., the betrothed's spending the night together), but also the sins of the parents or heads of families who allow such disorders.

Thus one understands the meaning in the other writings of the terms *conversari* (to dwell, live with), *ad domum accedere, in domo excipere, far all'amore.* Besides, we know from contemporary documents that "this rather common abuse—youthful cohabitation—gave many headaches to the civil and religious authorities." [52] This explains the pastorally cryptic statement in

Praxis (200): "Once the engagement has been celebrated, the espoused and their parents are in a state of mortal sin for the entire time until the marriage takes place.

Alphonsus is an intractable probabiliorist with respect to the proximate, unnecessary occasions of formal sin. One is bound in conscience, he says, to assure (tutiorism) that God will not be offended and that the penitent will not be lost. Hence this distinction:

> In general and if Christian prudence suggests it, the confessor ought to use a tolerant opinion. But if these tolerant opinions increase the peril of formal sin—as in the case, for example, of proximate occasions for sin—he is obliged as a physician of souls to uphold those opinions which are most certain to guide penitents into remaining in a state of grace.[53]

Alphonsus tolerates flirting (*"qui se invicem adamant"*) and dating which allow young people to get to know and appreciate each other in view of an eventual marriage (*Praxis* 65). What he rages against is cohabitation, which, he says, ninety-eight out of a hundred times is practiced by *sponsi*, fiancés, between their official engagement and their marriage. He had to be severe against this almost universal immorality in order to defend precisely the honor and good beginning of a Christian marriage worthy of the name.

SAINTLY MERCHANTS

Alphonsus wrote, "God wishes that all become holy, and each in his own state, married people in the state of matrimony" and, he adds, "merchants as merchants."

Just as shepherds in the time of Jesus were classified as sinners because it was believed that they sent their sheep onto other people's fields, so in the eighteenth-century merchants were treated as usurers by profession. Tutiorists, rigorists, and probabiliorists were in agreement that the sacraments should be withheld from merchants, business people, and "manufacturers" of every kind. To speak of holiness for money-grubbers was absurd!

Strengthened by his knowledge of business and his experience with humanity, Alphonsus was able to say to them, as he had said to married people, "You are called, as merchants, to holiness and are invited to daily Communion."

NO TO PROSTITUTION

The worst kind of immoral behavior at that time in the city and in the Kingdom of Naples was prostitution. The everlasting question was and is "Can it, or can it not, be tolerated?" In theory, everyone agrees; but morality is a practical matter. Therefore, is prostitution to be regulated as a lesser evil, prohibited, or abolished? The problem is taken up again and again by governments and by the churches. It is a question on which Catholic moralists have repeated ad nauseam a shortsighted tolerance up to the middle of the twentieth century. "A courageous exception," writes Charles Chauvin, "was Saint Alphonsus Liguori."[54]

"Can prostitutes be tolerated?" asks Alphonsus in his *Theologia Moralis*, and he replies:

A "probable" opinion responds in the affirmative, with Saint Thomas and other doctors. Saint Augustine clearly adheres to this way of thinking. Suppress prostitutes, they say, and worse sins will occur: sodomy, pollution, not to speak of the danger to which honest women will be exposed. Saint Augustine goes so far as to say, remove prostitutes from human society, and debauchery will throw it into total disarray.[55]

As usual, Alphonsus does not let himself be impressed by the great names. He is impressed only by arguments, but their arguments do not impress him on this point. From his long pastoral experience in the city of Naples in company with his disciple and friend the Venerable Father Gennaro Sarnelli, he sets forth "a more probable opinion" to challenge the lesser evil:

> The more serious ills which Augustine, Thomas, and the others feared are not to be avoided by tolerating prostitutes. Very much to the contrary, the passions of the lustful are stirred up by easy and frequent recourse to these women. Because vice grows with exercise, they never cease from committing pollutions and other abominations, in any case, with the prostitutes themselves. Nor will they keep from bothering honest women because of the prostitutes. Rather tolerance of prostitutes brings with it many other evils: prostitution of young girls, even by venal parents, waste of money, neglect of studies, more brawling, and scorn for honest marriage.

Later, it would take the medical studies of famous sexologists to bring the moral theologians Vermeersch (1919) and Salsmans (1925) to relinquish the inept theses of excessive tolerance and come to the side of Saint Alphonsus. Pius XII solemnly echoes them:

> The most formidable obstacle to your action [against prostitution] is neither the declared hostility of the enemies of God and souls, nor that of the libertines, nor that of the

traffickers in the white slave trade who shamelessly en-rich themselves. This hostility is completely understand-able....What is odd is that it is necessary to vanquish the careless, ironic, even indifferent Christians who believe themselves to be upright, convinced and practicing Catho-lics (September 1948).

Let us conclude. Was Alphonsus a derivative casuist or a bold innovator?

As a qualified representative of casuistry, Alphonsus should have been the preferred target of detractors of ca-suistical morality. He was, however, nothing of the sort. He enjoyed a warm and widespread sympathy among Catholic moralists of a progressive tendency. Alphonsus' moral theology, which might have suffered in the reac-tion against casuistry, in fact found itself placed within the group in favor of reform.[56]

Because, in his day, Alphonsus was sometimes an inspired, and always a courageous reformer.

CHAPTER 7

INFLUENCE AND
CONTROVERSIES

W hen he received the eighth edition of his *Moral Theology* in October 1779 at the age of eighty-three, Alphonsus put down his pen as a worker does his tools at the end of the day. To Giuseppe Remondini he wrote: "Many thanks for the beautiful *Moral Theology* you have republished. Had I left this world before its publication, I think I would have died unhappy."[1]

Nothing changed in the ninth edition (1758). Alphonsus was nearly blind and was barely able to see it. Thinking he was alone, he dared utter this dazzling prayer: "Lord, you know well that all that I have thought, said, done, or written, all has been for souls and for your glory."

He died at Pagani on August 1, 1787, while the noon angelus bells struck, with his spiritual sons, the Redemptorists, weeping by his side. Only eight months later, at the insistence of the people and clergy, the bishops of Nocera dei Pagani and Sant'Agata dei Goti began the cause for canonization.

"MY MORAL THEOLOGY HAS SPREAD EVERYWHERE"

On June 16, 1756, thirty years earlier, Father Liguori wrote to the same man, Remondini, about what was the culmination of his *Moral Theology*, the *Pratica del Confessore*:

> As you have let me understand, if you intend to spread this *Pratica* into Germany, Spain, etc., you must have it translated into easily understood Latin, since foreigners will not want anything of the Italian. This *Pratica* has received a universally warm welcome [in Italy].[2]

As was the case with all of his writings. On July 30, 1772, he again wrote to his publisher:

> My *Moral Theology* has spread everywhere. What of it if in Portugal it has been prohibited because of hatred for the Jesuits! In Naples no moral theology sells as well as mine, in spite of the proverb, "No one is a prophet in his own country."[3]

We note the reception in Portugal, which would not open its arms to Alphonsus until the end of the last century. But the rest of the Catholic world would accord him a triumphant welcome. In all, his works would go through twenty-thousand editions in at least seventy languages. Of his two principal moral works alone, *Theologia Moralis* would be republished fifty-eight times after his death, and *Homo Apostolicus* (*Istruzione e Pratica*) eighteen times during his lifetime (thirteen times in Italian) and seventy-four times after his death (thirty in Italian).

Was it a triumphant and instantaneous reception? No, it was a slow penetration by means of, sometimes, century-long struggles.

In Italy the moralist of the just mean was violently attacked, first from the right, then from the left. In the decades following his death, the fiercest opposition continued to be that of the Jansenists; especially those of the north—of Piedmont and Lombardy. Their leader, Pietro Tamburini (1738–1827) from Brescia —not to be confused with the Jesuit Tommaso (1591–1675) of the same name—began by spreading a rumor of a deathbed retraction by Alphonsus. Fairly quickly, the attack was stopped by the veneration in which almost the whole of the peninsula held Bishop Liguori. Bishops and important personages zealously sided with the saint and his teachings. The *Annali ecclesiastici*, which had opened its pages to a violent polemic against Alphonsus, finally had to recognize angrily on June 29, 1792, that "the most recent Holy Father of probabilism" was already in everybody's hands.

From 1820 on he was taught at the Minerva in Rome.[4] Fifty years later Alphonsus was attacked on his left flank by the probabilist Antonio Ballerini in a long drawn-out and very well-known debate that we will discuss later. Between these two dates we find the objections raised by Antonio Rosmini (1797–1855) in his *Principi della coscienza morale* (1831) and his *Trattato della coscienza morale* (1839).

Rosmini, a fervent priest and a prolific writer of immense culture, was the greatest Italian philosopher of the nineteenth century. His attempts to reconcile the dogmas of the Church with the requirements of philosophical reason—*his* philosophical reason—gained him the condemnation of forty of his propositions by the Holy Office.

He spun his philosophy on his solitary walks. All the *things* he met seemed to him to be nothing but the presence of a more general reality common to all—the idea of being, or Being itself. The first of his propositions to be condemned should be enough to give us an inkling of his philosophy:

In the order of created things there is manifested *immediately* to the mind something that is in itself divine, that by its essence belongs to the divine nature.[5]

It is in this intuition of the Divine Being that the intelligence grasps the objects of experience. In October 1885, the *Civiltà Cattolicà* characterized Rosmini in the saying: "Rosmini is a Jansenist in theology, a pantheist in philosophy, and a liberal in politics." Rosmini paid tribute to his "greatly beloved Saint Alphonsus," this "holy moralist whom I not only venerate, but whom I commend to everyone as the best of all the moralists." Nevertheless, he claimed to correct him on the essential functioning of thought:

Whoever looks closely will see that even though I object to certain *logical inexactitudes* to be found here and there in his writings, I do not diverge from the basis and spirit of his teaching. For if the mind of the great man occasionally makes *mistakes in reasoning*, his truly great holiness soon comes to his aid and he corrects or retracts the error he had committed unaware.[6]

By recalling his philosophy, we can see that Rosmini maintains against Alphonsus (1) that there can never be invincible ignorance that would excuse sin; (2) that it is illogical to speak of a doubtful conscience because conscience is a practical judgment on the rightness of an action, whereas doubt is the suspension of judgment; (3) that principles must be universal and therefore cannot admit an exception without losing its status as a principle.

Throughout this book, we have seen what Alphonsus' answers to Rosmini would have been. He made no claim to be a philosopher. His moral thought is not the product of solitary walks. He did not meet *things*, but *people*. He did not classify them from afar nor did he begin from a metaphysical intuition of universal being. Alphonsus got to know people in the particular details of their lives.

Rosmini had not yet been born, however, when Alphonsus' gentle theology had already swept Turin, the capital of Piedmontese Jansenism, and had begun to spread throughout Europe. That was due to Nicolas Joseph Albert of Diessbach. Born into a Calvinist family in Berne on February 15, 1732, Diessbach later entered the army. He converted to Catholicism before his marriage in 1754. Widowed by 1758, he joined the Society of Jesus the following year. Ordained in 1764, and perfectly trilingual, he distinguished himself as a preacher of missions in Switzerland, and in Piedmont, both before and after the suppression of the Jesuits (1773). He was the missionary of upper Italy—as Alphonsus was of Naples.

In spite of meddling regimes, in 1778 and in 1782 Diessbach established two secret societies connected with the French *Aa* (*Associations*)—the Christian Friendship Association and the Priests' Friendship Association. These were zealous groups, teams devoted to evangelization through the press, especially through the spread of Bishop Liguori's works. He had understood that the then contemporary teachings of the holy bishop was the best antidote to Jansenism, unbelief, and immorality. The Friendships spread to Milan, Florence, and far beyond the borders of Italy. Diessbach himself was seen in France, Bavaria, Milan, and Vienna, where he was joined by the young Saint Clement Maria Hofbauer to whom he communicated his enthusiasm for the person and the works of the founder of the Redemptorists.

Diessbach died in 1798. His disciple Luigi Virginio (1756–1805) continued his work in inspiring the Friendships throughout Europe, and was succeeded by his favorite spiritual son, the venerable Pio Bruno Lanteri (1759–1830).

According to Virginio, who was in a position to know, Diessbach spread Alphonsus' *Theologia Moralis* "into various regions, chiefly Switzerland, France, Bavaria and other places in Germany." Lanteri and his "Friends" poured their money and their life-blood into flooding Piedmont with *Homo Apostolicus*. In 1815, with Luigi Guala, he founded and directed the Ecclesiastical College in Turin, where Alphonsus' moral theology was taught to Saint Giuseppe Cafasso, Don Bosco, and to many others.[7]

Except for the *Glories of Mary* (1774), Spain was in no particular rush to let the works of Saint Alphonsus be heard in Castillian. Nonetheless, it was here that the *Theologia Moralis* was published for the first time outside Italy (Madrid, 1792). The cultural ties between the two peninsulas had once again held good. Unfortunately, however, both of these works were censured by none other than the Spanish Inquisition. A cold shower to cool any publisher's enthusiasm!

The two trifling accusations brought against the *Glories of Mary* at the Tribunal of the Supreme Council (1791–1793 and 1806) are of no particular concern to us here except to mention that the first trial lasted two years and resulted in a suspended decision.

Two charges were also made against Alphonsus' moral theology. The first indictment, in 1761–1762, related to the *Praxis Confessarii*. It required the suppression of five paragraphs in which Alphonsus dared to discuss morals among married people, clergy and religious, and a brief sixth paragraph in which he denounced the parents for tolerating and their engaged children for practicing premarital sex.[8] These statements were qualified as "false, scandalous, erroneous, reckless in matters of morals, and injurious to the state of the Church."

And the second indictment? As the faithful went to Mass

they could sometimes read posted on the church door an *Edicto Expurgatorio* issued by the Tribunal of the Holy Office. On Sunday, February 12, 1804, they read under the usual heading:

We, the Apostolic Inquisitors against heresy and apostasy, by Episcopal, Royal, and Apostolic Authority...[then come the list of] books, treatises and papers which may occasion the ruin of souls and which we order to be forbidden or expurgated, as the case may be.

In the category of works to be expurgated we find the "*Theologia Moralis* of the most illustrious Alfonso de Ligorio," Book VI, number 257 (Gaudé IV, p. 224). Just what was this scandalous affirmation that it was necessary to erase "on pain of major excommunication" because it "could cause the ruin of souls"?

On the question: If, after confession, one remembers a sin which one has involuntarily forgotten to confess, is it obligatory to go to confession again before receiving Communion? One opinion, very common among the doctors, says yes. Another stubbornly denies it, while [the laxist] Diana, usually more tolerant, also refuses it and refers to a decision of the Spanish Inquisition which ordered it be expurgated from the works of Padre Cornejo. *In spite of that, it seems to me absolutely reasonable.*

Here is the unfortunate sentence which Alphonsus ought to have kept his pen from writing and which had to vanish "under pain of major excommunication." According to the condemnation, "It is dangerous in practice." When the Inquisition takes a stand, it is forever and ever.[9]

Thus this condemnation was posted on the doors of the

churches on February 12, 1804. On May 18, 1803, however, the Holy See, after a rigorous examination, had published a decree affirming in the name of the Church that it had found nothing to censure (*nil censura dignum*) in all of Alphonsus' writings! This information had still not arrived in Madrid in 1806 when the same Supreme Tribunal censured the *Glories of Mary* for a second time.

Tired of royal or ecclesiastical censors, the diocesan or national Inquisitors, Bishop Liguori occasionally let drop such sayings as, "There is nothing to be done! Whoever publishes must be patient or die trying (*se non vuol morire crepato*)."[10]

Let us beware, however, of identifying Spain with its Inquisitors. Saint Alphonsus also had many problems, debates, and frustrations with the Neapolitan censors. If some Spaniards were nitpicking, it must be remembered that Spain was the first country outside Italy to publish his *Theologia Moralis*. It would be thirty years before other countries felt the need to do the same.

Nor should we forget that the Remondinis, father and son, in Venice and Bassano, were one of the world's largest commercial presses. Their books were distributed throughout Europe and beyond, even to China. Even during his lifetime, Alphonsus' moral theology was used by the graduates of Naples' Chinese College, where Alphonsus himself had studied from 1729 to 1732.

The Germanic lands were in no hurry to publish the complete *Theologia Moralis*. They could import it from Venice. But they were the first to extract its heart or essence, the *Praxis Confessarii*, to publish it during Alphonsus' lifetime at Augsburg and Innsbruck (1763, 1771) and at Laibach in Austria (now Ljubljana in Slovenia) in 1768. While he was alive, *Homo Apostolicus* appeared in Augsburg in 1774.[11]

It should not be imagined that German rigorism collapsed before Alphonsus as if they were the walls of Jericho. In the latter half of the eighteenth century the "immortal Concina" found a large audience in the Germanic countries influenced by the puritanical and pessimistic atmosphere of the Lutheran Reformation. But this audience has been exaggerated,[12] while the Alphonsian stream has been underestimated. Indeed, it was in Germany that many priests who had been uprooted by the French Revolution and the Napoleonic wars would discover Alphonsus' gentleness. When Riegler, in 1836, took Alphonsus for a Jesuit, he only demonstrated a gross, although commonly shared ignorance. Had not Napoléon Landais in his *Dictionnaire* (1834) defined the word *Redemptorist* as an archaic term for "A Jesuit in disguise"? Confusing Jesuits with Redemptorists, from which Alphonsus had already had to defend himself in order not to vanish with the former, was constant throughout the nineteenth century. None of this prevented the Bishop of Sant' Agata from writing to Giambattista Remondini on March 2, 1773:

A foreigner in the Kingdom writes to me that my work of moral theology has received a warm welcome in Germany; the same is true of my spiritual books, of which a number have been translated into German.[13]

In fact, by that date, eleven of his ascetical works had been published in German. This shows that, even before his death, Alphonsus was one of the chief guides and inspirations for those people that the "new history" now studies—the Christian populace and their pastors in the Germanic countries.

Alphonsus, however, was virtually ignored by the universities until around 1840. There are a number of reasons for this. The great university professors remain in the rarefied intellectual atmosphere of their books, their teaching chairs, and their abstract discussions, while Alphonsus, also university-educated and rigorously logical, wrote his *Moral Theology* to train missionaries and confessors. For university professors, the *Theologia Moralis* and its various reworkings belonged exclusively to the realm of casuistry, and not to that of science. According to them, it was at the opposite pole of the Enlightenment (*Aufklärung*): "Science appeals to principles, and not to simple rules of prudence," wrote a professor of Tübingen. Furthermore, the kind of systematic theology they were promoting was rooted in the contemporary philosophy of Kant rather than that of Descartes or of Thomas Aquinas. And by then new moral situations had also developed. One sought in vain in Alphonsus for advice on the important questions of the nineteenth century, such as obligatory military service, the use of chloroform, or vaccination. More profoundly, a gap separated northern liberal theology from "ultramontanist" Roman Catholicism. This explains the tension between the great Johann Michael Sailer (1751–1832), who had left the university for the bishopric of Ratisbon, and the Redemptorist Saint Clement Maria Hofbauer (1751–1820). We need also to consider that the Germanic mind is not the Latin and still less the Neapolitan, and Alphonsus was "the most saintly of the Neapolitans and the most Neapolitan of the saints."

Nevertheless, toward the middle of the nineteenth century, the wind had shifted in the universities toward scholasticism, casuistry, and "Liguorism." In 1839, the year of Saint Alphonsus' canonization, the Franciscan Adalbert Waibel published the first of eight volumes of his *Moral Theology according to the Spirit of Saint Alphonsus Liguori*. The Redemptorists Michael Heilig at Mayence in 1845, and Michael Haringer at Ratisbon in 1846–1847 simultaneously provided the Germans with a complete *Theologia Moralis* that had not been imported from Venice. At about the same time moral textbooks *ad mentem*

S. Alphonsi by Thomas Gousset, of the missionaries Jean-Pierre Gury, S.J., and Dieudonné Neyraguet, and of Pietro Scavini, rector of the cathedral and vicar general of Novara, pastors all, were published in Germany and began to interest specialists. Even better, university professors at Tübingen among other places began to recommend them warmly to their students.

Still, certain professors at Tübingen waged a long battle against Saint Alphonsus in the name of systematic science, German idealism, and what Hans Urs von Balthasar has called the "anti-Roman complex." This is not even to mention the anti-Jesuit campaign that painted Alphonsus and his congregation with the same brush. These attacks, although at first scattered, reached an unusual level of violence. Otto Weiss writes:

> The storm against the moral theology of Saint Alphonsus began only in 1868. It should be stressed that it was at first directed not against Alphonsus himself, but against Gury and the adoption of his textbook at the Grand Seminary of Mayence. The criticisms were refuted not only by the professors of the Grand Seminary but by Bishop Ketteler who explained his position in a pamphlet. Soon, however, Gury had to undergo a new assault, this time in Switzerland. Lachat, the bishop of Basel, came to Gury's defence, declaring that his textbook followed a moral theology approved by the Holy See whose author was "the immortal Saint Alphonsus Liguori who was endowed with an astonishing erudition." In spite of this, under pressure from the civil authorities, the book had to be withdrawn from the diocesan Grand Seminary.

Two years later, in 1871, in connection with the elevation of Saint Alphonsus to the rank of Doctor of the Church, a full-scale campaign was launched against him. The timing was not mere coincidence. The reaction aroused in

Germany by the dogma of infallibility, the beginnings of the
Old Catholic movement, and a number of measures undertaken by the government of the Reich all signalled the
"Kulturkampf" which was also carried out in the name of an
enlightened "German science" and against dark "Roman-
ism" and "Ultramontanism." Not by chance was the attack
launched by a man who had become the spokesman for
the opposition within the German church, namely, Ignaz
von Döllinger (1799–1890). Even before 1870 he had fought
for a German theology free of all foreign influences and
which could thus lay claim to the status of a science.[14]

On March 23, 1871, Alphonsus was proclaimed Doctor of
the Church. A few days later Döllinger left the Church. In 1889
he wrote with F. H. Reusch a *Geschichte der Moralstreitigkeiten
in der katholischen Kirche zeit den 16 Jahrhundert [History of
Moral Controversies in the Roman Catholic Church from the
16th Century]* in which he attacked Alphonsus and his moral
theology.

This was the signal for a campaign of defamation against
Saint Alphonsus, who was accused of immoralism. These petty
quarrels led some scrupulous confessors to think they had to
inform themselves indiscriminately on every detail about precisely those matters which Alphonsus had prescribed discre-
tion.

Other quarrels that spread far beyond Germany from around
1865 to 1930 arose over Alphonsus' moral system. Each side
laid claim to the Doctor of Moral Theology. These were academic quarrels, rearguard skirmishes, in which a prioris often
took the place of objectivity. Much paper was wasted. I once
read on a Belgian ashtray, "Before you write a word, remember the beauty of the blank page."

As O. Weiss says:

Two more things: As for the professors, there were several rare German moral theologians who, going beyond the surface of an historically conditioned casuistry, penetrated to the heart of Alphonsus' moral theology.

As for the pastors and the people of God, the great German Lutheran historian Adolf von Harnack (1851–1930) noted at the end of the nineteenth century, not without a certain amount of resentment, that

At the very moment when the Society of Jesus was suppressed, God raised up a new champion of probabilism and assured for it a future triumph on which, humanly speaking, no one would have counted. That champion was Alphonsus Liguori, the founder of the Redemptorists and the most influential Roman theologian since the Counter-Reformation.*

Beatified (1816), canonized (1839), Doctor of the Church (1871), Liguori was the exact antithesis of Luther and has assumed in modern Catholicism the place of Saint Augustine....Even if he stands far above the shameless probabilists of the seventeenth century, he nevertheless fully accepts their system and in an incalculable number of questions—even divorce, perjury, and murder—he knows how to transform the unacceptable into venial sins. No Pascal rose up against him in the nineteenth century. On the contrary, his authority as the new Augustine grows from year to year. He rules today in every religious orders, every seminary, in every textbook on morality.[15]

---

* Liguori and Voltaire were exact contemporaries and they were, far above all, the two spiritual leaders of the Latin nations.

This impassioned statement, which is too condensed to contain any necessary qualification, is nonetheless the work of a master of the history of dogma. Harnack was not afraid to compare Alphonsus with Luther, or with Voltaire, although in opposition to them both, or even especially with Augustine, the pessimistic and strict pastor of souls, who was replaced by Alphonsus' optimism and "laxity." The scale tipped very much in the Neapolitan's favor.

France did not experience the same university controversies. On the pastoral and seminary level, too, France seems to have been indifferent to Saint Alphonsus. But in the *Dictionnaire de théologie catholique* under the entry "Bailly," we read the following incredible summary, even more incredible when we remember in what high regard the French hierarchy had viewed Bailly.

BAILLY, Louis. Born 1730 near Beaune...died 1808. He produced a *Theologia dogmatica et moralis*, eight volumes *in octavo*, 1789, a work which has often been republished....Exhibiting a very rigid morality, in spite of later alterations in the definitive edition, this work, which was the textbook used for almost half a century in most French seminaries, was condemned by the Index on 7 December 1852 *donec corrigatur* [until corrected].

Such was the triumph of Alphonsian gentleness, but it was a slow and hard one, as the following passage from Father Burnichon shows:

The French clergy held on to their customs as to one of their privileges—and almost as if it were a dogma. It condemned with indignation any softening of its pitiless morality. The name alone of Liguori provoked its reprobation. He was held to be a dangerous, if not a positively heretical author—in any case, one formally excluded from seminary libraries.[16]

But as J. Guerber says:

We have not overlooked the "Friends" organized by Diessbach, Virginio, Lanteri and their wide and rigorous offensive on Alphonsus' behalf launched from Turin. Already by 1786, Luigi Virginio was teaching moral theology in the seminary of Saint Nicolas du Chardonnet in Paris where the teachers held anti-Gallican and anti-Jansenist attitudes.[17]

This was the first breakthrough. In a first-rate thesis, J. Guerber, S.J., studied and described "The Growing Support of the French Clergy for Alphonsus' Moral Theology" (*Le Ralliement du clergé français à la morale liguorienne*). We have only to consult this work, while remembering that he studied mainly ultramontanist authors, as his subtitle intimates: "The Abbé Gousset and his Precursors (1785–1832)." There were, however, other important authors: the Jesuits with Jean-Pierre Gury and his disciple, the missionary Dieudonné Neyraguet; Saint Eugene de Mazenod and his Missionaries of Provence, the Sardinian connection of Pierre-Joseph Rey, Joseph-Marie Favre, Pierre-Marie Mermier, and Bishop Bouvier....We cannot linger over these, but it would be a mistake not to mention them. Because many streams flow into the same river, it does not mean that their origins and pathways are the same.

Still, Thomas Gousset (1792–1866) headed the campaign. Guerber describes Gousset's efforts for the triumph of a cause he held most dear. In 1830, returning from a journey to Rome where he had make a vow to win this cause, he began teaching Alphonsus' doctrine at Besançon in spite of his colleagues' opposition. In 1831, he obtained a pronouncement from the Sacred Penitentiary that one could in complete security of conscience follow the opinions professed by Alphonsus. As vicar general, in 1832 he published in French a *Justification of the Moral Theology of Blessed A.-M. de Ligorio.* "This was a thunderbolt for the rigorist school; the book created a sensation," as the *Dictionnaire de théologie catholique* says. It was a great sensation which bore much fruit. Other teachers were won over by Gousset's courage. In the same year, Michel Thomas accepted the chair of moral theology at Langres only on the condition that he would be permitted to teach Alphonsian principles. Finally, in 1840, Gousset, now archbishop of Rheims, launched his *Compendium for the Use of Parish Priests and Confessors.* It was a practical résumé of Alphonsus' great *Theologia Moralis.* The book quickly spread throughout all of the dioceses of France. At the death of the Cardinal in 1866, it had reached thirteen French and Latin editions, with a number of others in various languages. It dealt a deathblow to Jansenist rigorism. In a letter of March 12, 1848, to Bishop Parisis, Montalembert hailed the change from "rigorism to Liguorism" a successful revolution of which the Archbishop of Rheims had been the apostle.[18]

The most conspicuous historical example of this change is the "conversion" of the patron saint of parish priests by the patron saint of moral theologians. Jean-Marie Vianney had been parish priest of Ars for fourteen years when Gousset's sensational work appeared. His spiritual father and teacher, the Abbé Charles Balley, a former canon of Saint Augustine and the parish priest of Écully, had trained him in Augustinian rigorism. *Sermon 78,* "On Absolution," from the first years of the Curé d'Ars' ministry contains the following passage that is almost a cry of despair:

Unless a complete change can be seen in us, without which we have not merited absolution, we have every reason to believe that we have committed a sacrilege. Alas, how few are those in whom this change can be seen after they have received absolution! My God, how many sacrileges! Oh, if only out of every thirty absolutions there had been a single good one, the world would soon be converted!

In his "first period," the Curé d'Ars thus felt himself obliged in conscience to defer many absolutions. His penitents, coming from afar and waiting days and even weeks for the forgiveness of God and the Church, thus made the fortunes of the innkeepers of Ars, Trévoux, and Lyons. But Gousset's *Justification of the Moral Theology of Blessed A.-M. de Ligorio* appeared in 1832. Bishop Devie of Belley, an enthusiastic follower of Alphonsus, recommended it to Vianney. It became a revelation for Vianney, revolutionizing his entire pastoral practice of the sacrament of penance. There were no more delays for absolution. And there were no more good times for the region's innkeepers. Vianney confessed: "Truly, how can I be severe to people who have come from so far, who have made so many sacrifices, and who are often obliged to disguise themselves in order to come here?"

Then his colleagues who sympathized with Jansenism accused this holy priest of laxism. Like his bishop, however, he had simply become a follower of Alphonsus. And he held more and more to this position. Every year from 1845 on he reread the volumes in which Cardinal Gousset had condensed Saint Alphonsus' moral theology.[19]

The reader may well ask, where were the Redemptorists during the battle for Alphonsian mercifulness in France? They arrived just in time to secure the victory. Only in 1820 did they establish their first house in France and it was in Bischenberg

(Department of Bas-Rhin), a German-language area. Not until 1831 were they established in French-speaking Tournai in Walloon Belgium.

When the Redemptorists arrived in the Netherlands—at Tournai (1831), Wittem (1836), Brussels (1841), and then Amsterdam (1850)—they were surrounded by practitioners of tutiorism. In the Netherlands, as elsewhere, the dogmatic errors of Jansenism had been disavowed in principle, while the rigorism that Saint Cyran, Arnauld, and Pascal derived from it was still practiced. Probabiliorism held sway in Louvain. As the future cardinal Van Roey wrote:

> For a good part of the nineteenth century, moral theology among us continued to be inspired by the rigorist principles that had prevailed in the previous century. Little by little, however, it began to free itself of this attachment and to adopt the teachings of Saint Alphonsus Liguori who had checked the Jansenist tendencies in Italy.[20]

It was during the turbulent years of the Revolution that the priests from the Netherlands, having fled to Germany, had the opportunity to discover and the time to study Alphonsus' moral theology. When they returned home, they became its prophets, so much so that copies of the *Theologia Moralis* imported "in large numbers" from Venice were quickly sold out and could not be found in the bookshops. The local publishers sensed a profitable opportunity here and printed the book at Malines (1822, 1828–1829, 1832, 1845–1846) and Anvers (1821–1823). Many separate editions of the *Praxis Confessarii* were published at Malines (1822, 1829, 1846, 1852) and Anvers (1823). *Homo Apostolicus* went through five editions at Malines between 1822 and 1842.

The purchasers were parish priests and religious, but not the seminaries. A professor at Malines declared: "He who follows Liguori is heading straight for hell." How could this faraway Neapolitan be right instead of their own Jansenius? Yet their resistance was not obstinate; it gradually crumbled away even at the University of Louvain between 1833 and 1844. In its Belgian edition of 1833, Gousset's *Justification* greatly helped to sweep away the opposition.

This time Alphonsus' Redemptorists took a hand in spreading his teachings.

As the Institute grew the number of studentates [schools] increased. By 1828 there were two more: one in Fribourg, Switzerland, and the other in Lisbon, Portugal. A fourth was opened in Saint-Trond in Belgium in 1833, but the number of its students increased so rapidly that in 1836 it had to be moved to Wittem [Holland]. The last named became the most important studentate of the period. Its location at the crossroads of the main routes into Belgium, the Netherlands, and Prussia made it the international seminary of the Transalpine Redemptorists. Among its first professors were the future Cardinal August Dechamps; Father Bernard Hafkenscheid, one-time rival of the future Leo XIII at the Gregorian University in Rome, who had been sought for a chair at Louvain by Msgr. van Bommel, and Father Heilig who in 1845 brought out the first new edition of the *Theologia Moralis* of Saint Alphonsus.[21]

At the same time, Redemptorist missionaries were evangelizing the region, and their apostolic work became a means for propagating Alphonsian morality. It was their habit during missions to meet the local priests who had been asked to help with confessions. The Redemptorists would explain to them the principles of Saint Alphonsus the Redemptorists were applying.

Since often ten and sometimes even twelve confessors were called upon to assist, after three or four years a large number of clergy were thus initiated. And this occurred in the best possible way to show them the practicality of these principles. Thanks to this tactic, instituted without any other motive but the success of the mission, a great many clergy were won over.

It might be said that toward the middle of the nineteenth century the name of Alphonsus Liguori dominated moral and pastoral teaching in Belgium and Holland.

Let us end our European tour in England and Ireland. Aside from the understandable opposition of the Dominicans—one's theology as usual being determined by the color of one's habit—Alphonsus appears to have entered these countries more easily then elsewhere. He was universally known in the nineteenth century, followed by many, accused of laxity only by some.

Newman (1801–1890), who did not admire him without some reservations, nonetheless wrote:

As Father Faber already thought, we are more and more convinced by the general judgment that he is the Doctor for the present age. Indeed, his moral theology has spread everywhere.[22]

Perhaps it was Philip Neri who reconciled this great liberal oratorian with Alphonsus.

From a somewhat different perspective, Cardinal Henry Edward Manning (1808–1892) said the same thing. Preaching at Clapham (London) in 1887 on the centenary of Alphonsus' death, he uttered these famous and true words of praise:

Doctor of the just mean, his influence on hearts has ever increased....This influence has passed from one nation to another, from one church to another, from one diocese to another, from one confessional to another. The spirit of Alphonsus and the gentleness of his pastoral love for souls have penetrated everywhere and have triumphed in all Catholic countries. Today they hold sway over the entire Church of God.

DOCTOR OF THE CHURCH

When Manning spoke, Alphonsus had for sixteen years been a Doctor of the Church and especially in moral theology, as we noted in the first chapter, the "Doctor of the just mean."

Alphonsus' reception had been such that some wanted him made a Doctor even before his canonization. The idea resurfaced in 1839. With seventy-four others, Bishop Mastai-Ferreti of Imola signed the request. Nevertheless, as Pope Pius IX, he was not particularly keen on the idea when Father Nicolas Mauron, the superior general of the Redemptorists, proposed it to him on July 23, 1867. On September 11, Mauron returned to his request bolstered with the signatures of 39 cardinals, 10 patriarchs, 135 archbishops, and 544 bishops. With the 75 signatures on the petition made to Gregory XVI in 1839, that made 803 signatories. Pius IX sent the file to the Sacred Congregation of Rites, and it began to make its way through the machine. The details do not concern us here except as they relate to moral theology, which, however, was the main "trial."

In this case, the opposition did not come from the Dominicans, but from the Jesuit Antonio Ballerini, professor of moral theology at the Roman College. On November 3, 1863, in his formal lecture beginning the academic year, he dealt with the moral system of Saint Alphonsus. In substance he said:

Those who are most familiar with Alphonsus are not in agreement on his moral system. Some present it as equiprobabilism or "a moderate probabilism," while others frankly assert that it is probabilist. Now, in his *Dissertations* of 1749 to 1755, he clearly declares himself to be a probabilist; nor did he who retracted so many things ever, whatever one may say, renounce his probabilism.[23]

There were rumblings among the Redemptorists. Their founding father had been made out to be nothing more than a Jesuit "wannabe."

To make matters worse, the Prosecutor for the Faith, Pietro Minetti entrusted Ballerini with writing the whole of his prosecution's "devil's advocate" speech. Ballerini, who in 1863 had so clearly understood Alphonsus' moral system, now declared it incomprehensible:

> Would you dare to exalt a doctrine which on the most important point entangles itself in so many and such great equivocations and teems with so many questionable elements?[24]

All the succeeding objections against Alphonsus the moral theologian were drawn explicitly from the criticisms that the Jesuit had recently made (in 1866) in his *Adnotationes* to a new edition of Gury's *Compendium Theologiae Moralis*. It was Ballerini himself who wrote the objections while they were signed by Minetti, and on thirty-four occasions the objections were backed up with a *Vide Ballerini* (see Ballerini). It was as if this eminent professor were the rule to which must conform anyone claiming the title of Doctor of the Church. One may be amused at these references to himself without in any way detracting from his merit or his title as the nineteenth century "Prince of the Moralists."

The 509 official pages that refute him are explicitly called the *responsa ad difficultates a clarissimo P. Antonio Ballerini, s.j., objectas.* To write the reply, the "Defender of the Case," professor Ilario Alibrandi, consulted a group of Redemptorist theologians.[25]

This confrontation was the height of what has been called the "Liguorian question." The most eminent theologians of both camps exhausted themselves uselessly in defending their own ideas of what Alphonsus thought about his moral system. What is important, however, is that Ballerini's barricades were pulled down and "the doctorate of Saint Alphonsus in 1871 marks a date in the history of moral theology" (L. Vereecke).

THE AUTHORITY OF SAINT ALPHONSUS

Alphonsus' authority grew as everyone began to quote him. Aside from Tanquerey, whose objectivity is unsurpassed, most contemporary authors of their own *Institutiones Morales* tried to wear Alphonsus' mantle. Pulled by both the right and the left, in spite of himself, he had to be a'' things for all people: a probabilist for the probabilists and a probabiliorist for the probabiliorists.

On May 18, 1803, after a scrupulous examination lasting several years, the Sacred Congregation of Rites conferred upon all the writings of Alphonsus the judgment *nil censura dignum* ("nothing to be censured") which then opened the way for his beatification.

"But that doesn't apply only to his moral theology," someone may object.

"True, but it also applies to his moral theology."

"But all servants of God whose cause has been introduced undergo this examination. It is a way of sifting them out."

"True again, but ever since Benedict XIV who established the rules, which moralist could claim to be so trustworthy? And

145

that the Holy See has proclaimed that he practiced the virtue of prudence to a heroic degree?"

In 1831, Cardinal de Rohan-Chabot Archbishop of Basançon, urged by his vicar general, the future Cardinal Gousset, submitted two questions to the Sacred Penitentiary: (1) May a teacher of theology adopt with complete confidence and teach the opinions which the Blessed Alphonsus Liguori teaches in his *Moral Theology*? (2) Must we caution a confessor who follows all of the opinions of Blessed Alphonsus Liguori in the practice of the sacred tribunal of penance only because the Holy See has found that there is nothing to be censured in the works of the Blessed One?

The reply to the first question was yes, with the qualification that one may follow different opinions if they have solid authorities behind them. This is a necessary qualification. To a concrete moral question there cannot always be one right answer. The plurality of the Gospels at the heart of a single Revelation establishes this as an affirmation of faith. The Holy See has condemned neither probabilism nor probabiliorism, but only their excesses.

The response to the second question was that a confessor can follow Alphonsus blindly.

But Alphonsus' opponent can still say, "That adds nothing to the *nil censura dignum*. As for the second response, I agree. As for the first, I don't. To say that Alphonsus can be taught "with complete confidence" has a quite different implication from saying that he cannot be censured.

In the end, however, let us remember the papal words of praise quoted in the first chapter about the Doctor of the "just mean" and the Patron of Moral Theologians and Confessors.

CHAPTER 8

SAINT ALPHONSUS TODAY

On November 25, 1971, in the Great Hall of the Alphonsian Academy in Rome, Cardinal Gabriel-Marie Garrone gave a lecture to celebrate the centenary of the doctorate of Saint Alphonsus. He began by saying:

> It is generally conceded that there is a "purgatory" for authors. After a sometimes prolonged period of great favor, a more or less long period of relative silence ensures, after which they are rediscovered with renewed enthusiasm.
>
> Has Saint Alphonsus now entered this "purgatory" that, unlike divine Purgatory, has nothing to do with justice?
>
> Perhaps, if one thinks of the prodigious success of the innumerable works of the Saint, of the unheard-of role that they have played in the development and deepening of Christian faith and piety for more than a century. An untold number of souls have fed on them and have been nourished in their fervor; and, no doubt, the birth and development of many religious Institutions have more or less consciously been inspired by them. In comparison, one must speak today of a relative eclipse. But one must also recognize that Saint Alphonsus finds himself in good company in this "purgatory." Waiting to be revived with

him are *The Imitation of Jesus Christ* and the *Devout Life*, great works which are often compared to the works of Alphonsus, showing the influence of the Saint. Truly, the crisis extends beyond a given author; it is a crisis of the spiritual life itself. That is in a sense much more serious, but is in nowise to the detriment of our author or his future.

Thus one may feel confident that a rediscovery of Saint Alphonsus Liguori will come. Does it not seem to be the case for Saint Francis de Sales, who is so close to Saint Alphonsus both in his inspiration and by the solemn recognition of the Church that has made them both Doctors?[1]

In fact, Alphonsus as a writer of spirituality and on Mary has already left purgatory. But what of the moral theologian?

TO CONTINUE THE REDEEMER'S WORK

University professors were mistaken if they did not understand that the *Theologia Moralis* and its spinoffs were not written for them, but for missionaries. Did not Alphonsus himself repeat it often enough?

These missionaries worked within a careless, often sacrilegious Catholic Christendom where the Church and the State made strange bedfellows. The principle that everyone was a practicing Christian stood firm. Today's era is completely different.

And many of our problems are also completely different, running the gamut from nuclear energy to bioethics. What would Alphonsus have to say about the contradictions found at the very heart of our values: about science, the arms race, prenatal diagnosis, and so on?

But is not the main concern of a moralist, who is also a believer, always the glory of God and the salvation of souls? Is it too much to ask that one's head and one's heart be given over to the passion of continuing the work of the Redeemer? Alphonsus writes:

> Dear reader, my intention in writing this *Moral Theology*, which has a strictly practical goal, was not to present you with a thick, scholastic treatise on "human actions." *Rather, wanting to help with the salvation of souls*, I believed myself obliged to choose solely those questions which, in this area, we deem the most necessary and useful to know for *the conduct of life*. Had I acted otherwise in my studies I would have wasted both my lamp oil and my efforts; and you, dear reader, would be wasting your time in reading such useless writings.[2]

Th. Deman finds our moral theologian's purpose odd:

> One would be completely mistaken to seek here a complete and systematic moral theology. Saint Alphonsus keeps far from claiming this, caring only, he says by a curious process of reasoning, for the salvation of his reader and that of other souls. This justifies a displacement of moral theology to highlight questions of conscience, a displacement which we have criticized above.[3]

A displacement? Whose fault is it if not that of the Redeemer, the teacher and guide of the Redemptorist Alphonsus Liguori? Does not His example call to us today? Especially if the chief source of a "complete and systematic moral theology" is the Revelation found in the Scriptures? Chief, but not unique. Chief inasmuch as Revelation itself justifies reliance upon the intelligence for establishing moral norms and solving specific problems.

Scripture Alone? Yes and no

On October 30, 1971, at the time of the centenary of Alphonsus' doctorate, Cardinal Villot, the papal Secretary of State, wrote a letter to the Archbishop of Naples on behalf of Pope Paul VI. He referred to the Council (*Optatum totius* 16) in the following terms:

> Moral theology must above all else direct itself to the Holy Scriptures. There it will find its fundamental theme developed: namely, "The nobility of the Christian vocation of the faithful." There it will discover the riches of the mystery of Christ and those of a theological anthropology which will enable it to understand the profound reality of the Christian. There it will find the principles that involve the whole person: continual conversion of oneself, living in the faith and love of the Father, imitating Christ, living as a redeemed and regenerated person in faith and in the sacraments. There it will find the fundamental values and attitudes—disinterested love, justice, willingness to bear the cross and so on—that the selfish person would willingly ignore. There it finds the Sermon on the Mount where Christ himself describes the person who belongs to the Kingdom of God. There, finally, moral theology will find, for example in Saint Paul, the attempts of the first Christians to establish concrete moral norms applicable to the community.

Not only would Alphonsus have signed this text with his own hand, he wrote it with his whole life. He approved of these sentiments especially in the little treatises on the moral requirements of holiness which he published in 1754 and 1755 while he was breaking through Busenbaum's hold on him by rewriting his *Theologia Moralis* and adding his *Pratica del Confessore*.

But it should definitely be remembered that Alphonsus did not find the concrete directives that moral theology needs for specific cases in the Gospels. To develop directives, he called for good judgment and extensive knowledge:

He who wishes to administer the sacrament of penance must first acquire the necessary learning to exercise this great ministry. It is the art of arts, as Saint Gregory wrote. And Saint Francis de Sales said that the office of confessor is the most important and the most difficult. This is true. It is the most important because it is the end of all the sciences: namely, eternal salvation. It is the most difficult because, first, it requires familiarity with almost all of the other sciences and with all of the crafts and professions; secondly, moral science touches upon many different kinds of subjects; thirdly, it is comprised for the most part of positive laws each of which is to be understood in its own particular sense.[4]

Great and indispensable casuistry!

But Alphonsus' adversaries, with Concina at their head, are also as much casuists as he—without knowing it:

As Father Deman shrewdly remarks, Concina, after having denounced the excesses of the probabilists, in turn undertook to construct a countercasuistry the details of which were in no way inferior to the models of the genre. In his monumental moral theology, Concina also had to deal with a multitude of moral problems which he strove to solve in his own way.[5]

Could there be any other way? There has been no other possible method in ethics since antiquity, nor will there be until the end of time. In 1987, Father Paul Valadier wrote:

> Morality does not consist in beginning with supposedly well-established principles and then deducing coherent practical consequences from these principles. Aristotle already warned against the erroneous confusion of practical with speculative reason. He insisted that moral reasoning proceeds by making a concrete judgment about an equally concrete situation. This implies much greater courage and determination than would be required if one could simply follow a sure deduction from principles.[6]

Were he alive today, Alphonsus would also add that, faced with new and complex problems that are springing up everywhere, the Church's learning and competence and its best qualified confessors will be at a loss. They will have to call humbly upon the competence and moral sense not only of specialized laypersons, but of nonbelievers. Solutions, however tentative, will emerge only from multidisciplinary cooperation in which biblical scholars will play only a part and the Church will only play her part. Did not the Second Vatican Council show us that this was the way to proceed?

> In fidelity to conscience, Christians are joined with the rest of humanity in the search for truth, and for the genuine solution to the numerous problems which arise in both private and social life.[7]

It is no longer enough to start with basic moral theology—especially when we are no longer living in the age of Christendom. For the majority of our contemporaries, the Bible and Christian morality are only one ideology among others.

As repositories of divine truth, the Churches… forget that they are included in the rejection of the great ideological systems.

John Paul II would like the secular powers to impose the Church's morality on everyone, believers and unbelievers alike. The Church has not behaved otherwise about divorce, contraception, or abortion. In every case it has hoped that legislation will forbid for the whole population what the Church forbids for its faithful. In this, the Church is like many other religions, from Islam to Judaism, which likewise reject lay pluralism when circumstances are in their favor. Even in America, we see fundamentalists— more Protestant fundamentalists than Catholic—putting pressure on the government to enact as law their vision of good and evil. The principle is always the same: a Church tends to see in its morality a "natural" rule valid for all humanity.[8]

The problem is not to know whether or not the Church is right. The result in either case is that the Church is rejected, sent back to its rectories, and all dialogue is broken off. The rest of the world cries, "Catholics, keep your Catholic morality for yourselves and let us live our own lives!" Being essentially a missionary, Alphonsus Liguori would trust in the fact that every human being is shaped in the image of Jesus Christ. Refraining from futile appeals to biblical, Christian, and patristic morality, he would speak in a language understandable to people today, a language of reason and conscience, a language for which he had once been so criticized.

CONSCIENCES NEEDED

Alphonsus' position was upheld by the texts of the Second Vatican Council:

Man is obliged to follow his conscience in all his activities....He is bound to obey his conscience...even if it should happen that it errs through invincible ignorance.[9]

Thus Alphonsian morality is organized around two poles of interest: to study how the *judgment of conscience* has to operate and to determine its application in the *practice of confession*. Alphonsus' morality belongs to the "moral theology of conscience" and the "moral theology of the confessional." Conscience and confession are the two poles of his moral doctrine.[10]

CONFESSORS NEEDED

Nothing could be more contemporary than conscience. But confession?

In 1969, Father Bernard Bro, O.P., published an opportune book with the provocative title *Sinners Needed* (*On demande des pécheurs*). In it he says: "Owing to a lack of enthusiasm on the part of the faithful and to weariness on the part of the priest, confession today is shunned or abandoned" (p. 26).

Certainly, had Saint Alphonsus lived before the Fourth Lateran Council he could have been in and for his time the same dogmatician and great spiritual father that we know. He could have written his wonderful little moral treatise, the *Pratica di amar Gesù Cristo*, as a commentary on Saint Paul's hymn to charity. But he would not have been able to write the "confessor's guide" that is in essence his great *Moral Theology*.

From the thirteenth to the twentieth century, the pastoral situation united salvation canonically and exclusively to confession and to the absolution of sins. This situation conditioned Alphonsus as a missionary and as the founder of a Congregation of missionaries. By force of circumstances and his vocation, his *Moral Theology* is welded to the confessional and, consequently, to what is permitted and what is forbidden. But it also provided him with the occasion to introduce to the confessional a new emphasis on the Gospel's message of Christ's love for all people, especially sinners. His equiprobabilism sought at once to protect the Pauline freedom "that Christ has given us" and to avoid the slippery slope of a probabilism that could lead to a laxism whose law would no longer be love.

Proclaiming Alphonsus heavenly patron of confessors and teachers of moral theology, Pius XII in 1950 justified this significant promotion in the following words:

He educated in a perfect way a very great number of confessors and he desired most frequently to sit on the tribunal of penance for the forgiveness of sins. Moreover, he assigned the religious of the Most Holy Redeemer whom he had assembled into a Congregation that their chief task was to hear confessions. Lastly, he left, both in speech and in writing, for the education and direction of confessors a remarkable moral and pastoral teaching which has been the most highly esteemed in the whole world up to our present age, often and highly recommended by the Sovereign Pontiffs as a most sure guide for ministers of the sacrament of penance and for spiritual directors.[11]

But there it is—sinners are needed! The baptized have abandoned the sacrament of reconciliation *en masse*. Because of a lack of sins? Clearly not. Because of a lack of a sense of sin?

Certainly. But without doubt also because of a lack of confessors.

By not taking the work of "reconciliation" seriously, we now entrust almost anyone to hear the short *pro forma* confessions, just before the major holidays, or the repetitive weekly confessions, or to give the general Easter absolutions granted to miserable lives which there is no question of improving.

It is enough to read a few chapters of Alphonsus' *Moral Theology* to see two things. The first is that, for him, individual reconciliation took a long time—like a consultation with a physician. The *New Rite of Reconciliation* describes only one rite for the individual reconciliation of a penitent and, fortunately, it is a long rite. Why, then, do the most official documents appear to be unaware of this? Can the bishop of Sant'Agata dei Goti help us to remember it?

The second thing that Alphonsus stresses over and over again is the need to educate confessors. Time and again, he insisted that they be knowledgeable. And available.

How can the priest be free from sin who through laziness neglects to hear confessions or fails to be able to hear them...? Priests are obliged to provide for their neighbors those things necessary for their salvation....Given that such an exercise is a work of charity, it is nevertheless a work that has as its motive not a simple motive of charity but the proper work of priest, to which...this obligation is added by virtue of divine institution; it is an office which he is bound to do when necessary for the people. Vainly would one excuse oneself from it on grounds of deficiency and weakness....Saint Francis de Sales labels false the so-called humility of those who refuse to use the sacrament for the salvation of souls because of what they claim to be their knowledge of their own weakness....The truly humble man, by contrast, is courageous because he does not rely upon his own strength at all, but puts his trust in God.[12]

Patient and helpful confessors are also required:

A confessor is shirking his duty when he sends away uninstructed people, telling them that they ought to examine their consciences. This is an inexcusable error...because people of this sort will vainly trouble and exhaust themselves trying to examine themselves sufficiently when the priest would do better to perform the examination himself. On the contrary, he should greatly fear that if he sends them away, they will be discouraged by the difficulty of examining themselves and will stay away from confession and wallow in their sins. This is why the confessor must himself examine them, asking them questions according to the order of the precepts. This is especially true if they are farmhands, carters, drivers, domestic servants, soldiers, bodyguards, innkeepers, or other such people who are accustomed to living a life that neglects their salvation and ignores the things of God because they do not often attend church and still less frequently hear preaching. The delusion of sending away some of these ignorant people to examine themselves may be even greater...for it is greatly to be feared that they would no longer return to confession and would be lost.[13]

Also needed are discreet and sensitive confessors who are concerned with the whole life of the penitent without becoming inquisitorial torturers:

Above all, the confessor will devote himself to knowing the state of his penitent, that is, his manner of living, how diligent he is in his work....The confessor must be careful not to show too much solicitude or anxiety to know exactly the definite number of sins, or even to make a definite judgment. He must be satisfied with ascertaining in a general way how often lapses occur and from there making an approximative judgment by taking the sins for what they are in God's sight....As for the rest, after he has made two or three questions, the confessor should little trouble himself if he seems to have only an unclear idea of the judgment he ought to make since it is morally impossible to hope for greater clarity from confused and disordered consciences.[14]

Finally, confessors are needed who believe, like Alphonsus, in the efficacious grace of the sacrament and to put their trust in it:

For the habitual sinner of good will, absolution will bring a most powerful assistance from God. His amendment is thus much more likely to come from the grace of the sacrament than from delaying absolution. It will make him stronger and will add to the effectiveness of the means he will use to root out his bad habit.[15]

On the subject of delayed absolution, Alphonsus twice writes something that could only come from a saint.

In canon 961 of the present *Code of Canon Law* it is stated that, among other cases, collective absolution may be given to penitents who would be deprived of the sacramental grace or of holy Communion for a lengthy period of time.

How would our saintly lawyer interpret this "lengthy period

of time"? We know that a priest in a state of mortal sin cannot administer a sacrament without making himself guilty of a grave sacrilege. Alphonsus therefore asks:

> Can one ask absolution of a priest who is in a state of mortal sin? Some authors answer yes, if the penitent as a result of not receiving absolution would himself be reduced to remaining for a lengthy period of time in a state of mortal sin.

What does "for a lengthy period of time" mean? Alphonsus replies, "An hour, for it is most important to be freed from sin at the earliest opportunity."[16]

Since we are discussing the relevance of Saint Alphonsus for our time, let us also recall (1) his theology of grace and of prayer, without which the moral life or holiness would be impossible; (2) the importance he attributes to Communion as the sacrament of forgiveness, strength, and life; and (3) the liberation he brings to marriage, anticipating sections 30 and 31 of the Second Vatican Council's document, *Gaudium et Spes*.

Let us leave the last word, however, to Leo XIII who, writing to the bishops of Italy on December 8, 1902, called Alphonsus "the most eminent and the gentlest of moralists."[17]

GLOSSARY

Anticurialism See Curia.

Attrition

Imperfect contrition wherein sorrow for sin does not have the love of God as its predominant motive, but rather fear of the punishment which the sin merits.

Casuistry

The art of resolving "cases" of conscience, that is, concrete and complex situations in which conscientious people may find themselves.

Certitude

The state of mind which adheres firmly, without fear of error, to an assertion taken as true. *Physical* certitude is based on the laws of nature; *moral* certitude on an interior evaluation which is either intellectual or psychological.

Conscience

The practical judgment of reason declaring what one can and cannot do according to the moral law. According to Alphonsus, the conscience is *sound* if it is in the right, *mistaken* if it is in the wrong. The latter is *corrigibly mistaken*, and thus guilty, if it suspects its error but makes no effort to escape from it; it is *incorrigibly mistaken* if it errs in good faith. That conscience is *broad* which habitually interprets the precepts of morality in the most liberal sense; *narrow* when it interprets them in the strictest sense.

Curia
The assemblage of persons and services that, under the authority of the pope or bishop, make up the government of the universal Catholic Church (the Roman Curia) or a diocesan church (the episcopal or diocesan curias). *Anticurialism* is the opposition to the power of the Roman or episcopal curia, which is deemed to be intrusive.

Duty
The obligation to do or not to do something on the strength of one's conscience or of lawful authority.

Equiprobabilism
The moral system according to which when a law has, as far as one can judge, equal probabilities both for and against it, it imposes no obligation because it has not been promulgated.

Equity
The superior sense of justice that leads to fulfilling the law in its spirit, beyond the letter and sometimes even against the letter.

Freedom (moral)
Permission to follow one's own personal choice not determined by an internal or external law. Not to be confused with *free will*.

Free will
The faculty of choosing for one's self, for good or evil, without constraint.

Gallicanism
Doctrine and practice emanating from the Church of France and claiming a certain independence in relation to the Holy See of Rome. The opposite of *Ultramontanism.*

Jansenism
A heretical doctrine of grace whose chief proponent was Cornelius Jansen or Jansenius (1585–1638). It maintains that human nature was completely corrupted by original sin, that predestination is absolute with certain persons being destined for hell and others for heaven, that grace is irresistible, that Christ died only for those predestined for salvation. These errors were condemned by Urban VIII in the Bull *In eminenti* (January 19, 1643), Innocent X (1653), and Clement XI (1713). Jansenism taught a rigorous morality and asceticism that drove people away from the sacraments.

Laxism
A theological and pastoral trend which allowed, in morality, freedom to follow every opinion enjoying a minimal or even doubtful probability.

Law (moral)
A prescription by nature, conscience, or authority considered as expressing the will of God.

Law (juridical) (in the sense of the body of positive law)
The official rules in force in a political society (customary, civil, or criminal law) or a religious society (canon or ecclesiastical law). In the eighteenth century, ecclesiastical law was made up of the collection of the canons (rules) of the Councils and of the Decretals of the popes. *Natural* law is that which is derived from the nature of things.

Moral theology
The science dealing with how human beings must use their free will in order to accomplish good and avoid evil.

Opinion
The assent of the mind based on signs of truth that are not scientifically demonstrated, but which render it apparently true, without excluding, however, the possibility that these signs might be delusory. In the latter case, a false opinion is considered true by the person who maintains it. Every opinion that exhibits a serious sign of truth is said to be *probable*, even if its contrary exhibits one that is more serious. An opinion that exhibits signs of more or less equal strength to its contrary is called *equiprobable* (or what Alphonsus calls the *truly probable* opinion). An opinion that exhibits signs of truth clearly stronger than those of its contrary is *more probable*, even though the contrary opinion has considerable signs of truth.

Penance (sacramental)
The act of reparation imposed by a confessor on the person who confesses his sins and receives absolution. The sacrament of penance is currently called the sacrament of reconciliation.

Probabiliorism
The system of morality according to which one is obliged when in doubt to follow the more probable and surer opinion even if the contrary opinion is almost as possible.

Probabilism
The system of morality according to which, in cases of doubt, the more probable choice is not considered binding when there is a probable opinion against it.

Probability
The quality of a thought or act that possesses some sign of truth. It is *intrinsic* if this sign comes from the very nature of the thing in question; *extrinsic* if it depends upon the authority of an author or recognized witness.

Rigorism
Moral severity, whether in the imposition of harsh obligations, parsimony in the forgiveness of sins, or the requirement of extraordinary conditions for receiving the Eucharist.

Sensus fidelium
Literally: the common opinion of the faithful. It is the shared thought of a large majority of the faithful on a matter of faith or morals. On Pentecost the Spirit was poured out on the whole people of God.

Sin
A conscious and free violation of the will of God. A *material* sin is an act, though evil in itself, that is committed by someone who is not aware of the malice pertaining to it. A *formal* sin is an act which is judged, whether rightly or wrongly, by the person who does it as being contrary to the law of God. Only the latter

is truly sin, and is always so, because sin belongs to the conscience. A *venial* sin is an offense against God but does not deprive the sinner of grace. *Mortal*, variously called *grave*, *serious*, or *deadly* sin destroys grace and causes the supernatural death of the soul, because it is a turning away from God.

Tutiorism
A system of morality used when there is indecision about the existence or nature of a law. It is deemed always necessary to choose the surest course (namely, that of the law's requirements) even if a contrary opinion is more probable.

Ultramontanism
Literally: "beyond the mountains" *ultra montes* (that is, to the south of the Alps in relation to the rest of Europe and especially France). The doctrine and practice which consists of affirming the absolute power of the pope over the universal Church. Opposite of *Gallicanism*.

NOTES

Introduction

1. Gaudé, vol. I, p. xlvii.
2. Ibid., p. xlix.
3. *Documentation catholique* 47 (1950), col. 945.
4. P. Colletta, *History of the Kingdom of Naples, 1734–1825*, trans. S. Horner (Edinburgh and London, 1858), Bk I, chap. 1, section xii.
5. P. Chaunu, *La Civilisation de l'Europe des Lumières* (Paris, 1971), p. 286.
6. Chaunu, pp. 397–398.
7. Ibid., p. 405.
8. On the Caravita academy and its leaders, see Dino Carpanetto and Giuseppe Ricuperati, *L'Italia del Settecento,* crisi, trasformazioni, lumi (Bari, Laterza, 1986), chaps. 7–8.

Chapter 1

1. Cf. T. Rey-Mermet, *Alphonsus Liguori: Tireless Worker for the Most Abandoned*, trans. from the second French edition by Jehanne-Marie Marchesi (Brooklyn, 1989), p. 134.
2. Francisco Marin-Sola, *L'Évolution homogène du dogme catholique*, trans by Basile Cambou, (Second edition, Fribourg, 1924), vol. 2, p. 195. Originally *La evolución homogénea del dogma Católico: Introducción general sobre el autor, la obra y la "nueva teología" de Emilio Sauras* (Madrid, 1923).
3. A.D. Sertillanges, O.P., *La philosophie morale de saint Thomas d'Aquin,* new ed. (Paris: Aubier, 1942), p. 401.
4. This section relies upon two works by Professor J. Delumeau: *La Peur en Occident XIVe–XVIIIe siècles* (Paris: Fayard, 1978) and *Le Péché et la Peur: la culpabilisation en Occident* (Paris: Fayard, 1983) translated as *Sin and Fear: The Emergence of a Western Guilt Culture 13th–18th Centuries* by Eric Nicholson (New York: St. Martin's Press, 1990). Cf. also F. Ferrero,

167

"*Angustia religiosa y moral cristiana en el siglo XVIII,*" *Moralia* (Madrid) 33:51–64.

5. Pascal, *Les Provinciales,* Letter 11. Biblical quotation: Proverbs 1:26.

6. Origen, *Homilies sur le Levitique* (Paris, 1981), II, 4.

7. John Cassian, *Conferences,* XX, 8.

8. J. M. R. Tillard, O.P. "*La pénitence sacramentelle: une théologie qui se cherche,*" *Studia Moralia* 21 (1983):15–16.

9. Canon 7 of the Council of Trent on the sacrament of penance.

10. J. Delumeau, *Sin and Fear,* p. 315.

11. DS, n. 812–813.

12. DS, 1709.

13. "*Maxime quae ad confessiones audiendas videbuntur opportuna.*" Quoted in Vereecke, p. 504, n. 29.

14. Vereecke, pp. 28–29.

15. *Ratio Studiorum,* Regulae Provincialis, 19, ¶4.

16. Cf. Louis Cognet, *Le Jansénisme,* series "Que sais-je?" (Paris, 1961); J. Delumeau, *Catholicism Between Luther and Voltaire: A New View of the Counter-Reformation,* (London and Philadelphia, 1977), pp. 99–128.

17. Vereecke, pp. 575–576.

18. DS, 2102.

19. Louis Vereecke, "*La théologie morale du concile de Trente à saint Alphonse de Liguori,*" *Studia Moralia* 25 (1987):19.

20. Vereecke, pp. 578–579.

Chapter 2

1. Antonio Tannoia, I, pp. 4–5.

2. Tannoia, I, p. 7.

3. Tannoia, I, p. 7.

4. Ambrogio Freda, C.Ss.R., "*S. Alfonso universitario,*" in *S. Alfonso de Liguori: Contributi bio-bibliografici* (Morcellanea, 1940), pp. 109–110.

5. Prospero Lambertini, *Annotazioni sopra le feste di Nostro Signore e della Beatissima Vergine* (Bologne, 1740), I, xxi. Quoted by S. Majorano, C.Ss.R., in *Studia Moralia* 9 (1971):118.

6. *Lettere,* II, p. 495.

7. *Lettere,* III, p. 623.

8. Quoted by Antoine Degert, *Histoire des séminaires français jusqu'à la Révolution,* 2 vols. (Paris, 1912), II, p. 227.

9. Louis Vereecke, "*La théologie morale du concile de Trente à saint Alphonse de Liguori,*" p. 31, p. 21.

10. On Genet, cf. James A. Pollock, S.J., *François Genet: The Man and His Methodology* (Rome, 1984).

11. Ibid., p. 256.
12. Cf. A. Degert, ibid., pp. 227–231.
13. *Riposta apologetica ad una lettera d'un religioso...,* ed. Corbetta (Monza, 1831) in *Apologie e confutazioni,* I, pp. 111–112.
14. Cf. Romeo de Maio, *Società e vita religiosa a Napoli nell'età moderna (1656–1799)* (Naples, 1971), pp. 25–26.
15. Giuseppe Sparano, *Memorie storiche per illustrare gli atti della Santa Napoletana Chiesa,* 2 vols., (Naples, 1768), vol. I, pp. 241–44, 315.
16. Cf. Giuseppe Cacciatore, S. *Alfonso de Liguori e il giansenismo* (Florence, 1944), p. 374.
17. *Dell'uso moderato dell'opinione probabile,* ed. Corbetta (Monza, 1831), pp. 283, 425.
18. Tannoia, I, p. 39.
19. *Dissertationes quatuor,* ed. Marietti (Turin, 1829), pp. 69–70, 231–232, 345–346. Tannoia, I, p. 39.
20. Luke 1:17
21. Tannoia, I, p. 39.
22. Cf. Rey-Mermet, *St. Alphonsus Liguori: Tireless Worker for the Most Abandoned,* pp. 194–198.
23. The notebook is in the General Archives of the Redemptorists (AGR) in Rome. Reference SAM VI 10. A second notebook, which we shall deal with later, continues the present one into the 1750s.
24. Acts of the Apostles 9:8–19.
25. Luke 10:16.
26. Cf. especially Psalm 119.
27. *Anti-Memoirs,* translated by Terence Kilmartin (New York, Chicago and San Francisco, 1968).
28. On the *Cappelle serotine* see Rey-Mermet, pp. 173–183.
29. *Adnotationes in Busembaum* (Rome, 1757), I, pp. 23, 56.
30. *Homo Apostolicus,* Finis Auctoris, p. iv.
31. Gaudé, I, p. lvi.

Chapter 3

1. Cf. Maurice de Meulemeester, *Bibliographie générale des écrivains rédemptoristes,* Vol. I: *Bibliographie de S. Alphonse-M. de Liguori* (The Hague-Louvain, 1933).
2. R. Coulon, "Concina," in *DTC,* III, col. 705.
3. Cf. Andreas Sampers, *"Controversia quam S. Alphonsus sustinuit 'de maledictione mortuorum,'"* in *SH* 14 (1966):3–47. Cf. also Gaudé, I, pp. 447–459; Tannoia, I, pp. 185–186; Raymundo Telleria, *San Alfonso Maria de Ligorio,* 2 vols. (Madrid, 1950), I, pp. 405–409.

4. The *Pii Operai* were closely connected with Saint Alphonsus. His uncle, Bishop Giacomo Cavalieri, and the future Bishop Falcoia, his second spiritual director, were members. See the excellent article in the *Dictionnaire de spiritualité.*

5. *Homo Apostolicus,* tr. V, n. 10.

6. *Riposta a un'anonimo* (1756), beginning.

7. His original German name is Busenbaum, but in Latin and the Romance languages the apposition of the consonants *n* and *b* is difficult. In the title of his work in Latin, his name is therefore Busembaum in almost every edition. Cf. Sommervogel, *Bibliothèque de la Compagnie de Jésus.* Saint Alphonsus often italianizes the name as *Busembao.* We have adopted Busenbaum.

8. Letter published in the journal *S. Alfonso* (Pagani) 12 (1941):198–200.

9. Tannoia, I, p. 245.

10. On Alphonsus' choice of Busenbaum, and for a detailed analysis of his work, see F. Ferrero in *SH* 23 (1975):293–365. Cf. also the magisterial work of Vidal, pp. 46–54.

11. Giovanni Olivieri, who was converted by Alphonsus, played a great role in his life.

12. Tannoia, I, p. 245. In his dedication to Benedict XIV Alphonsus explained the need for a second edition by the "universal success" of the first. It had sold out.

13. Gaudé, I, p. lv.

14. *Lettere,* I, pp. 260–261.

15. Tannoia, I, pp. 245–246.

16. *Lettere,* III, p. 477.

17. Tannoia, I, pp. 247–248. Cf. Ferrero in *SH* 23 (1975):364–365. We do not know what Iorio's question was.

18. *Lettere,* III pp. 141, 144–145.

19. Ibid., III, p. 420; *SH* 17 (1969): 373–380; Gaudé, I, p. xxiv.

20. *Lettere,* III, p. 40.

21. Cf. de Meulemeester, p. 122.

Chapter 4

1. F. Genet, *Theologia Moralis* (Venice, 1705), cap. 1, quest. 4–5.

2. Cf. Vidal, pp. 126–134.

3. *Praxis Confessarii,* n. 17. Gaudé, IV, p. 536.

4. *Dissertatio scholastico-moralis pro usu moderato opinionis probabilis* (1749), in *Dissertationes quatuor* (Modoetiae, 1852), cols. 70–71.

5. *Riposta ad una lettera d'un religioso circa l'uso dell'opinione egualmente probabile* (1764), vol. I, (Monza, 1831), cols. 100–102.

6. Gaudé, I, p. 3, n. 1 and 2.

7. Ibid., p. 4, n. 6.

8. Ibid., pp. 155–156, n. 174. Cf. *Lettere,* III, pp. 246–247.
9. Tannoia, I, p. 246.
10. Gaudé, II, pp. 52–53.
11. *Homo Apostolicus,* tr. I, n. 79.
12. Gaudé, II, p. 54.
13. Tannoia I, p. 247.
14. Cf. C. Damen, C.Ss.R., "*S. Alphonsus doctor prudentiae,*" *Rassegna di morale e diritto* (Rome), 5–6 (October–March 1939–40): 1–27, p. 6.
15. J. Maritain, *Distinguish to Unite, or, The Degrees of Knowledge,* translated under the supervision of Gerald B. Phelan (New York, 1959), p. 463.
16. D. Capone, *L'Osservatore Romano* (29 March 1981), p. 7.

Chapter 5

1. Thus the *DTC* instead of an article on "Probabilism" imposes on us a not always well-informed argument *against* it.
2. General Archives of the Redemptorists (AGR), SAM VI, 9a.
3. Austin Berthe, C.Ss.R., *Life of Saint Alphonsus de'Liguori: Bishop and Doctor of the Church, Founder of the Congregation of the Most Holy Redeemer,* trans. Harold Castle (St. Louis, Mo., 1906), I, p. 454; Félix Delerue, *Le Système moral de saint Alphonse-Marie de Liguori* (Saint-Étienne, 1929), pp. 37–40.
4. Telleria, I, p. 557.
5. *Lettere,* III, p. 20.
6. Ibid., pp. 23–24.
7. AGR XXVII, 8.
8. *Lettere,* III, p. 27.
9. Quoted by F. Delerue, p. 39.
10. Cf. Louis Vereecke, pp. 582–588. See also Gaudé, I, pp. 25–70 for Alphonsus' exposition of his *Morale systema.*
11. Servais Pinckaers, O.P., *Ce qu'on ne peut jamais faire* (Fribourg, 1986), pp. 128–129. My emphasis.
12. Michel Labourdette, *Revue thomiste* 58 (1950):230.
13. *Lettere,* III, p. 130.
14. Ibid., pp. 167–168, 170.
15. Ibid., pp. 176–177.
16. Ibid., pp. 205–206.
17. Ibid., pp 333–334. "Assassins and rebels"? The sinister Pombal accused the Jesuits of the attempt on the life of the king of Portugal, who was wounded on the night of September 3–4, 1758. When you want something done, any excuse will do.
18. Enrica Viviani della Robbia, *B. Tanucci et il suo più importante cartegio* II (Florence, 1944), p. 119.

19. *Lettere*, III, p. 343.
20. Ibid., p. 344. Cf. pp. 297–298.
21. Ibid., pp. 421–422.
22. Contrast this with what R. Coulon in the *DTC*, III, cols. 705–707, s.v. "Concina," says. Coulon disingenuously separates out individual phrases and, moreover, appears to be unaware of the historical context in which the subtlety of Alphonsus' thought evolved. He even seems unaware of the substance of the explanations. On this debate, cf. Delerue, pp. 50–57; *Studia Moralia* 2 (1964):89–155, and 3 (1965):82–105.
23. *Lettere*, III, p. 477.
24. Cf. Vereecke, pp. 588–593.

Chapter 6
1. O. de Dinechin, "*L'éventail des éthiques*," *Cahiers de l'actualité religieuse et sociale*, no. 340 (1 December 1986): 8–9.
2. P. Hazard, *European Thought in the Eighteenth Century: From Montesquieu to Lessing* (New York, 1963, 1969), p. 336.
3. O. de Dinechin, pp. 9–10.
4. B. Häring, "*Sant'Alfonso: una morale per i redenti*," *Morale e Redenzione* (Rome, 1983), p. 23.
5. Gaudé, III, pp. 625–629.
6. *Homo Apostolicus*, Appendix IV, ¶1 (*Monita ad Confessarios*), XXI.
7. Ibid., tr. XVI, n. 108 et seq.; Gaudé, III, pp. 633–636.
8. Gaudé, III, p. 550.
9. *Modo di conversare...con Dio*, n. 11, 12, 36 in Eugene Grimm, C.Ss.R., ed., *The Complete Works of Saint Alphonsus de Liguori*, II, pp. 395, 398.
10. *Regolamento di vita*, chap. III, ¶V.
11. *Uniformità alla volontà di Dio*, in *Opere Ascetiche*, I, p. 286.
12. *Pratica di amar Gesù Cristo*, chap. VIII, section 10, in *Opere Ascetiche*, I, p. 79.
13. Quoted by J. Delumeau, "*Morale et pastorale de saint Alphonse: bienveillance et juste milieu*," in *Alphonse de Liguori Pasteur et Docteur* (Paris: Beauchesne, 1987).
14. John 8:11 and Luke 15:1–2.
15. Cf. Rey-Mermet, pp. 167–168.
16. Tannoia, III, p. 153.
17. Gaudé, III, p. 477.
18. *Homo Apostolicus*, Append. iv, xi.
19. Édouard Hamel, "*Retours à l'Évangile et théologie morale, en France et en Italie, aux XVIIe et XVIIIe siècles*," *Gregorianum* 52 (1971):676.
20. Tannoia, III, p. 153.
21. Ibid. I, p. 39.

22. Gaudé, III, p. 467.
23. Ibid., pp. 468, 470, 473.
24. Ibid., pp. 474–76.
25. Ibid., p. 477.
26. DS, 1692.
27. *Homo Apostolicus,* tr. xvi, n. 49.
28. Ibid., n. 51.
29. Ibid., n. 54.
30. Tannoia, I, p. 39.
31. Saint Vincent de Paul, *Correspondance, entretiens, documents* (Paris, 1920–25), III, pp. 369–370.
32. Cf. E. Dublanchy, *"Communion fréquente,"* DTC, cols. 542–46; G. Cacciatore, *S. Alfonso de Liguori e il giansenismo,* pp. 470–480.
33. Tannoia, II, p. 124.
34. Ibid., I, p. 332.
35. A. Di Meo, *Confutazioni della lettera e replica di D. Cipriano Aristasio* (Naples, 1764), pp. xxvi–xxvii. Quoted by Cacciatore, p. 477. On Di Meo, cf. M. de Meulemeester, *Bibliographie générale des Rédemptoristes,* II, pp. 125–126.
36. Gaudé, IV, pp. 612–614. Cf. *Homo Apostolicus,* Append. I, nn. 29–36.
37. *Homo Apostolicus,* ibid., n. 30.
38. Cf. Tannoia, II, p. 19; De Meulemeester, I, pp. 118, 123; *SH* 15 (1967): 113–125; Henri Boelaars, *"La polemica de S. Alfonso de L. sulla communione domenicale,"* Studia Moralia 9 (1971):321–340.
39. J. Delumeau, *Sin and Fear,* p. 220.
40. Cited by Delumeau, p. 27.
41. Cf. Rey-Mermet, *Ce que Dieu a uni* (Paris: Centurion, 1974), pp. 161–196; above all, see Vereecke, pp. 531–552.
42. Gaudé, IV, p. 95.
43. Ibid., p. 551.
44. Ibid., p. 82.
45. Ibid., p. 109.
46. Ibid., pp. 61–63.
47. *"Valide contrahitur cum intentione vitandi prolem,"* Ibid., p. 61.
48. *"Immo etiam aliquando simplici affectu licite excludatur, v. gr. a paupere, ne nimium prolibus gravetur,"* ibid., p. 109.
49. *"Vinculum perpetuum animarum cum obligatione reddendi debitum,"* ibid., p. 59.
50. I thank Fr. Vereecke for sending me this passage from a forthcoming article.
51. Gaudé, III, p. 459; *Praxis Conf.,* ibid., IV, pp. 562, 624; *Homo Apost.,* tr. VII, 32: tr. ult., 3; *Il Confessore diretto,* cap. XXI, 22 and 42; *Reflessioni*

utili ai Vescovi, cap II, 6: "*Del sinodo*"; *Istruzione al popolo,* cap. VI, ¶6, n.
6; Tannoia, II, pp. 60 and 328–329.
52. Cf. Tellería, I, p. 410 and n. 19; II, pp. 208–209 and notes; *Lettere,* I, p. 611;
Tannoia, *loc. cit.*
53. Gaudé, I, pp. 62–63.
54. Charles Chauvin, *Les Chrétiens et la prostitution* (Paris: Cerf, 1983), p. 65.
55. Gaudé, I, pp. 678–679. Cf. Tannoia, II, p. 328; *Lettere,* I, pp. 475–476, 512.
56. Vidal, p. 204.

Chapter 7
1. *Lettere,* III, p. 531.
2. Ibid., p. 37.
3. Ibid., p. 420.
4. Cf. G. Cacciatore, *S. Alfonso de Liguori e il giansenismo,* pp. 412–425;
Tannoia, III, pp. 81–83, 230–239.
5. *DTC,* XIII, col. 2929.
6. Quoted by Giovanni Velocci, C.Ss.R., "*Antonio Rosmine et S. Alfonso de
Liguori,*" *Studia Moralia* 25 (1987):117. I owe much to this article. The
emphasis is mine.
7. Cf. Cacciatore, pp. 425–430; Jean Guerber, *Le Ralliement du clergé français
à la morale liguorienne: l'abbé Gousset et ses précurseurs (1785–1832)*
(Rome: Gregoriana, 1973), pp. 171–182.
8. References in Tellería, II, p. 313, n. 46.
9. Cf. Tirso Cepedal, "*La inquisición española ante la moral de S. Alfonso
(1793–1804),*" *Pentecostés* 15 (1977):293–334.
10. *Lettere,* III, p. 387.
11. Bibliographic information here and elsewhere is taken from de Meulemeester, I.
12. J. Diebolt, *La théologie morale catholique en Allemagne au temps du
philosophisme et de la restauration, 1750–1850* (Strasbourg, 1926), p. 21f.
13. *Lettere,* III, p. 441.
14. O. Weiss, "*Alfonso de Liguori und die deutsche Moraltheologie im 19.
Jahrhundert,*" *Studia Moralia* 225 (1987):146. From this extensively
researched article I have drawn what I have written here about the German
academics.
15. A. von Harnack, *Lehrbuch der Dogmengeschichte* (Friburg-im-Br./Leipzig,
1894–1897), III, pp. 677–678.
16. Joseph Burnichon, S.J., *La Compagnie de Jésus en France: Histoire d'un
siècle (1814–1914)* (Paris, 1914–1922), III, p. 219.
17. J. Guerber, pp. 186–187.
18. Cf. Charles Guillemant, *Pierre-Louis Parisis,* (Paris, 1916–1924), I, pp.
239–241 and 198.

19. Cf. Philippe Boutry, *Prêtres et paroisses au pays du Curé d'Ars* (Paris, 1986), pp. 408–421; J. Cognat, *Vie de Mgr Alexandre-Raymond Devie, évêque de Belley* (Lyons, 1865).
20. *"Les sciences théologiques"* in *Le Mouvement scientifique en Belgique, 1830–1905* (Brussels, 1908), II, p. 520.
21. M. de Meulemeester, *Outline History of the Redemptorists* (Louvain, 1956), pp. 131–132. The present section on the Netherlands draws upon the *Bibliographie* of the same author and owes much to his *"Introduction de la théologie morale de saint Alphonse de Liguori en Belgique"* in *Ephemerides theologicae lovanienses* XVI (1939):468–84.
22. J. H. Newman, *Letters and Diaries,* XVI, p. 303, in Giovanni Velocci, *"Sant'Alfonso visto da Newman,"* *Rivista di vita spirituale* 40 (1986):176.
23. Ballerini's inaugural lecture was published in Rome in 1864: *De morali systemate S. Alphonsi M. de Ligorio dissertatio habita in aula maxima Collegii Romani.* It can be found in the General Archives of the Redemptorists (AGR) in Rome: BA 103, 32: n. 6.
24. *Acta Doctoratus,* III, p. 11.
25. Ibid., *Summarium additionale,* Proemium. On the history of this cause, cf. Giuseppi Orlandi, *"La causa per il dottorato di S. Alfonso,"* *SH* 19 (1971):25–240.

Chapter 8

1. In *Studia Moralia* 9 (1971):10.
2. Gaudé, II, p. 689.
3. *DTC,* XIII, s.v. *"Probabilisme,"* p. 582.
4. *Homo Apostolicus,* tr. XVI, n. 99. Cf. Gaudé, III, pp. 652–653.
5. É. Hamel, *"Retour à l'Évangile et théologie morale...,"* *Gregorianum* 52 (1971):677.
6. P. Valadier, S.J., *"Notre précarité, une chance pour la vie morale,"* *Christus* 134 (April 1987):136.
7. *Gaudium et Spes,* 16.
8. François de Closets, *"Qui détient les clefs de la morale?"* *L'événement du jeudi* (18–24 June 1987):54–55.
9. *Dignitatis humanae,* 3 and *Gaudium et Spes,* 16.
10. Vidal, p. 215.
11. *Documentation catholique* (1950):944–945.
12. *Homo Apostolicus,* tr. XVI, n. 127.
13. Ibid., n. 103.
14. Ibid., n. 103.
15. Ibid., tr. ult., n. 15.
16. Gaudé, III, p. 69. Cf. *Homo Apostolicus,* Append. III, n. 20, 3.
17. *Leonis XIII Pontificis Acta,* XXII (Rome, 1903), p. 253.

INDEX

Index

Index

Index